TEACHI

MW01673267

CTE-03

For

Certificate of Teaching in English [CTE]

Gullybaba.com Amazon.in GPHbook.com

BESTSELLER

Useful For

IGNOU, KSOU (Karnataka), Bihar University (Muzaffarpur), Nalanda University, Jamia Millia Islamia, Vardhman Mahaveer Open University (Kota), Uttarakhand Open University, Kurukshetra University, Seva Sadan's College of Education (Maharashtra), Lalit Narayan Mithila University, Andhra University, Pt. Sunderlal Sharma (Open) University (Bilaspur), Annamalai University, Bangalore University, Bharathiar University, Bharathidasan University, HP University, Centre for distance and open learning, Kakatiya University (Andhra Pradesh), KOU (Rajasthan), MPBOU (MP), MDU (Haryana), Punjab University, Tamilnadu Open University, Sri Padmavati Mahila Visvavidyalayam (Andhra Pradesh), Sri Venkateswara University (Andhra Pradesh), UCSDE (Kerala), University of Jammu, YCMOU, Rajasthan University, UPRTOU, Kalyani University, Banaras Hindu University (BHU) and all other Indian Universities.

Closer to Nature We use Recycled Paper

GPH BOOK®

GULLYBABA PUBLISHING HOUSE PVT. LTD.

ISO 9001 & ISO 14001 CERTIFIED CO.

Published by:
GullyBaba Publishing House Pvt. Ltd.

Regd. Office:
2525/193, 1st Floor, Onkar Nagar-A,
Tri Nagar, Delhi-110035
(From Kanhaiya Nagar Metro Station Towards Old Bus Stand)
Call: 9991112299, 9312235086
WhatsApp: 9350849407

Branch Office:
1A/2A, 20, Hari Sadan,
Ansari Road, Daryaganj,
New Delhi-110002
Ph.011-45794768
Call & WhatsApp:
8130521616,8130511234

E-mail: hello@gullybaba.com, **Website**:GullyBaba.com

New Edition

Price: ₹200/-

ISBN: 978-93-81970-90-4
Author: Gullybaba.com Panel

Preface

Teaching is both an art and a science. Able teachers always find ways and means to improve their teaching techniques. With the change in time, the teachers are asked to employ newer methods of teaching their pupils more effectively so that they must be able to cope with the demand of the age. The improvement of the teacher by employing newer methods of teaching and the latest techniques of teaching is a need of the hour.

The education system of any nation being shaped and likely to be shaped. Education has been and will continue to be the potential cause of change in any society. Education develops manpower for different levels of the economy. It is also the substrate on which research and development flourish, being the ultimate guarantee of national self-reliance.

This GPH book ***"Teaching Strategies (CTE-03)"*** provides various strategies of teaching to improve students' learning. The book is written in question & answer format to provide students with the instant gratification of a correct answer. We have tried to solve all possible questions from the exams' point of view. The book is enriched with useful and to-the-point matter. Previous year question papers have also been included to help students to understand the unique examination structure. We hope that this effort will fullfil the expectations of the readers and help them to excel in exams.

We wish you a successful and rewarding career with us. Feedback in this regard is solicited.

– GPH Panel of Expert

Acknowledgement

Our compliments go to the **GullyBaba Publishing House (P) Ltd.,** and its meticulous team who have been enthusiastically working towards the perfection of the book.

Their teamwork, initiative and research have been very encouraging. Had it not been for their unflagging support, this work wouldn't have been possible. The creative freedom provided by them along with their aim of presenting the best to the reader has been a major source of inspiration in this work. Hope that this book would be successful.

– GPH Panel of Expert

Publisher's Note

The present book of the CTE series is targeted for examination purpose as well as enrichment. With the advent of technology and the Internet, there has been no dearth of information available to all; however, finding the relevant and qualitative information, which is focused, is an uphill task.

We at **GullyBaba Publishing House (P) Ltd.,** have taken this step to provide quality material which can accentuate in-depth knowledge about the subject. GPH books are a pioneer in the effort of providing unique and quality material to its readers. With our books, you are sure to attain success by making use of this powerful study material. Provided book is just a reference book based on the syllabus of particular University/Board. For a profound information, see the textbooks recommended by the University/Board.

Our site **gullybaba.com** is a vital resource for your examination. The publisher wishes to acknowledge the significant contribution of the Team Members and our experts in bringing out this publication and highly thankful to Almighty God, without His blessings, this endeavor wouldn't have been successful.

– Publisher

Contents

Question Papers

1 General Principles of Teaching-Learning

An Overview

Institutions of higher learning across the nation are responding to political, economic, social and technological pressures to be more responsive to students' needs and more concerned about how well students are prepared to assume future societal roles. Faculty are already feeling the pressure to lecture less, to make learning environments more interactive, to integrate technology into the learning experience, and to use collaborative learning strategies when appropriate.

Teachers make a variety of decisions to promote learning. They decide on the curriculum, learning goals and objectives, and teaching methods. Within teaching methods, they decide on which instructional strategies they will use. One of the qualities of effective teachers is the knowledge and effective use of a wide variety of strategies. Instructional strategies are research-based tools that guide teachers in maximising student achievement.

Q1. What, according to you, would be a good language lesson? Provide its characteristic features.

Or

Briefly describe the key features of a typical language lesson.

Ans. Language is a term most community used to refer to called natural language –the form of communication considered peculiar to human kind. Language is a skill. It does not end up with knowledge of other subjects like Economics, History, Biology and a host of other subject, which operate at knowledge level. The content material of such subjects entails learning and its recall as and when required under controlled conditions. The knowledge of a language, its origin, nature, elements, usage, etc. is also learned in classroom teaching-learning situations. This learning, however, is theoretical and aims at introducing the language to the learners. But basically, a language is a skill-oriented learning; no knowledge of its theory would be good if the learner cannot apply it. Language, therefore, operates at a higher cognitive level, i.e. application. A language, therefore, is a communication skill. The primary aim of a language is communication in a social setting.

The teacher needs to develop the base material in the syllabus and course book into the processes of lesson. To some extent, the nature of the 'subject matter' influences the structure of (suitable) classroom lessons. The language has certain special qualities. For most school subjects, the course book provides, in a fairly detailed manner, the items of content (information, definitions, rules, theories) that are to be 'taught'. This involves presenting, explaining, demonstrating, etc. by the teacher so that this content is transmitted effectively to pupils and it become a part of their knowledge. For language (which we treat as a skill subject rather than a content subject), the value of such content (knowledge) in itself is rather limited. The main objective of the teaching-learning of a living language like English, is to help the learners to become able to use it to communicate with others, by sending and receiving meaningful messages. Formal knowledge 'about' the language is useful, but this cannot be the primary concern of language lesson. This is important for teachers of English. But surely the pupil in Std. VIII or IX does not need to 'know' all this technical information. Similarly, gaining knowledge and understanding of the ideas (content) found in passages, stories, poems that the course book contains is not a major aim in itself. Learning this content is primarily a means to the larger goal of becoming skilled in the use of English.

'Problem' arises here is that neither 'information' about the English language as a system nor the 'ideas' in passages, poems, etc. from the central core or backbone of the language curriculum. Language is learnt most successfully by experiencing its use. This does not mean that pupils have to talk and write (produce complex texts) most of the time. It means that during lessons, they should get a fair measure of exposure to and experience of language in use – similar to what the child acquiring a language naturally seems to get very easily most of the time. The stories, passage, poems, etc. in the course materials are texts of various types. The teacher helps pupils to engage with texts in such a manner that they experience how meaning is expressed or conveyed through the language they contain. The samples of language available even in a Std. VII or VIII level course books will include a wide range of selections. Among them, texts may carry descriptions of deeply felt personal experience, accounts of emotionally powerful interactions among persons (characters), expressions (in verse or prose) of joy and zest, or of sadness and weariness, parts of speeches or documents that have inspired and moved people, descriptions or explanations of 'technical' items that are clear and interesting even to the layman, pieces with hidden meanings that emerge only after much reading/re-reading and reflection...

The objective of language teaching (when we have brought learners together in a classroom) is not to 'transmit' the teacher's superior understanding and appreciation of such texts to pupils; it is rather, to help them experience or 'see for themselves' the meanings. Further, we would also want them to see how meaning is related to aspects of language, form or structure as demonstrated in the texts. It is interesting about such texts that they can (with some seriousness and sincerity) be approached from many perspectives. A whole range of 'question' can be raised directly or indirectly about a text: Who created it? Who is the sender/author? Who is addressed to? Why was it created? When? In what context/circumstances? Could the same 'message' have been conveyed in some other way(s)? What response might it have generated originally? Will other 'receiver' react in the same way? The point here is not that dozens of such trivial comprehension questions must be asked in relation to every 'passage'. These are not 'comprehension' question as such; they are rather, ways of approaching and responding to texts. For discussion, these questions/ approaches represent the principle that many tasks or activities can be taken up in class that would carry discussion far beyond the specific and limited aim of finding the meaning of the passage. The teacher of a content subject, who has to deal with a chapter with such matter, cannot afford to go into the open-ended question suggested above, even if pupils are willing. This is because the objective of instruction there is for pupils to get or learn the ideas in the passages. Similarly, in a linguistics class, such selected texts serve as data for studying the rules of the language. However (and here is the important principle), in a language lesson, such activities that take off from a given text, re-reading and reflection, dramatisation/role-play, renderings as picture/cartoon, composing continuations; etc. can be of value. They can provide many (perhaps not all) pupils with opportunities to engage and interact with texts following their own interests, attitudes and styles. There are no single 'right answers' to be produced or arrived at by all. Through such explorations, pupils might get a 'feel' for how 'language works' to express meanings in a variety of settings. The discussion and collaboration involved in such activities will also provide pupils with opportunities to use language purposefully to negotiate meaning.

The general principle for language instruction that emerges from this discussion is that the language lesson should provide for a variety of open-ended tasks demanding attention, effort and some measure of interaction on the part of all the pupils. Presentation and explanation of 'content' by the teacher (to which pupils 'listen') should be only one of the strands in the processes of instructions in the classroom, but not the dominant one. Possibly, it after this type of effort on the part of pupils, that explanation-analysis by the teacher (good old-fashioned pedagogy!) becomes really useful. Language lessons as we think of them now, have learner activity as a major and significant feature, and not merely something to be taken up (time permitting) after the usual presenting-explaining by the teacher has been done. However, 'learner activity' is not an end itself. Simply reducing 'teacher talk' will not automatically lead to language learning. Good language lessons do not simply happen; they have to be prepared and planned with great care. It is not only the 'what' and 'how' of presentation that has to be planned, but also 'when' and 'how' pupils are to be involved, and how what they do/produce can be built upon to create relevant learning experiences. The book you can believe most - GPH book.

Q2. Highlight the nature of learning experiences that can be generated during a classroom lesson.

Or

"One aspect of planning for lessons is the listing of a series of things that the teacher will do and pupils will do within the time restriction. The second is linked to pupil involvement and participation..." Comment on the given statement.

Or

Imagine you have conducted an experiment in your classroom to develop communication skills of your student. Describe the objective, topic/area, methodology, findings and follow up action taken by you. [June-2012, Q.No.-5]

Ans. Various classroom activities that make up lessons provide learning experiences. The term 'learning experiences' refers to what individual pupils might be perceiving, thinking, feeling, intending to do, attempting to do, while a lesson is in progress (and while doing homework, assignments, etc.). Such experiences undoubtedly are personal and private. No one else (like the teacher) can directly control them or order (demand) what they 'should' be. However, it is possible and reasonable to argue that certain types of teaching-learning activities would probably generate certain types of learning experiences. The materials (course book) represent one strand or layer of activities. Some of the activities commonly indicated in course books are: silent reading of short texts, re-reading of texts with specific purposes in mind, formulating responses to texts (explaining, predicating, relating to life), expressing them in speech or writing, working on language exercise, composing shorter or longer texts (written or spoken). Among the activities that the teacher can add or develop from the materials are: listening to teacher's presentations-explanations, reading aloud, write down notes (from teacher talk or blackboard), engaging in a discussion with the teacher (all students can be involved even if only a few actually speak), working on tasks/problems or discussing some issues in pairs or groups.

Many activities are possible during teaching. This abundance of possibilities for classroom 'operations' should remind us that when teacher talks, it becomes the predominant mode of activity in a lesson though many other possible and desirable things are not happening. Similarly, if twenty minutes or more are devoted to writing answers or compositions (silently and individually) other possibilities are being set aside. It is the need to choose from this large set of possibilities that makes planning and preparation for lessons virtually unavoidable. Planning by the teacher does not necessarily mean major deviations from the scheme given in the course book. Modern course books are well organised and contain a wide variety of activities. (After all, the syllabus designers and material writers have expertise library resources, and also time, in plenty!). The argument we are considering here is not that the course book is unsuitable, but that it is common and general, and hence, incomplete. Given the wide variation in pupil characteristics and classroom situations across schools, some units will not match or suit some groups of learners. This is where the teacher has to make conscious choices and decisions, based on her intimate knowledge about her class abilities, style and discipline/interest, and above all, their learning history, i.e. what they have and have not already learnt or been exposed to in earlier classes or in other subjects. Planning done with such information in mind will lead to a plan/scheme for a lesson or set of two or three that is tailor-made for each particular class. Other teachers also dealing with the same unit and topic, which will develop different plans. Thus, the essential part of planning is the selection by the teacher of activities (learning experiences) "most suited to my pupils now" from the large inventory of 'generally' good items available.

One aspect of planning for lessons is the listing of a series of things that the teacher will do and the pupils will do along with the time estimates. This would function like a detailed programme schedule. A second aspect of planning is linked to the emphasis we now place on pupil involvement and participation. As we know that some of what pupils do or produce can contribute to the lesson properly. How does this happen? One example can be found in the way composition classes are conducted sometimes. A broad theme or topic is taken up for preliminary discussion. Opinions and suggestions from pupils are invited and put up on the board with only minimal correction or editing. With this pool of ideas as a base, the focus and structure of the piece (paragraph, report, story, etc.) is agreed upon and the actual writing begins. Instead of the teacher simply 'giving' a topic and outline of points/hints (such complete writing exercises are found in course books), their ideas and suggestions are made a part of the preparation for writing. An idea that one pupil has, is made available to others. Individual pupils thus, contribute to the 'inputs' received by others as a part of the lesson, helping the teacher in effect. Thus, such a process of participation is open-ended and unpredictable in relation to planning. A class may find the proposed theme very exciting and virtually flood the teacher with their ideas; or they might be quite bored and unresponsive. In the former case, the teacher will have to manage the discussion skillfully and move to the next phase at an appropriate time. This has to be done sensitively. After inviting pupils to offer their ideas, it is unfair and discouraging to cut short the discussion suddenly, after only a few have spoken. The teacher needs to predict that 'what happens' and 'be prepared'.

Objectives of the Lesson: The following are general objectives of teaching "Translation".

- To elaborate students, "What the topic of translation is?"
- To provide the knowledge and understanding of the various aspects of translation.
- To enable students how translation helps in communication.
- To develop the abilities and skills among students to speak correct English language while communicating.
- To develop the linguistic ability among students and use in their own expressions.

Subject: English **Topic:** Translation

Methodology: The teaching of "translation" should be in the first year of the English course as soon as pupils acquire some measure of command over the language. But the translation taught to them should not be formal translation (which should be gradually introduced only when they are in third year, i.e. in class—VIII) only, rather it should be informal also. The purpose of teaching English during the first two years is to give them a command over the basic structures of the language. Hence, in the first year the translation they are taught should be in the form of function of words and the way they are used. Care should be taken that they do not get lost in the changing of meanings of the words and their definitions. They should be made familiar with the topic through imitation, practice and repetitions. For example, they can be taught how to structure a sentence, if they are made to imitate the teacher, practice and repeat the sentences such as:

राम लिखता है।	Ram writes.
मोहन के पास दो पेन हैं।	Mohan has two pens.

Findings: Now the students are able to translate. The topic serves as exercise in comprehension within students. It helps us (teachers) to test pupils understanding of the language English and make students to bring out differences from the mother-tongue. As we communicate every time, in any language we want, the skill of translation learnt at school can be of great help in this regard for L2 learners.

Q3. "In order to become an effective teacher... it is of paramount importance to be able to manage the classroom." Discuss how you will do so using pair and group work.

Or

Write a short note on Pair work and Group work.
[June-2011, Q.No.-1(a)][Dec-2011, Q.No.-1(a)]
[June-2012, Q.No.-1(e)]

Or

Write a short note on Fixed pairs and flexible pairs in pair work activities. [Dec-2010, Q.No.-1(b)]

Or

Do you agree with the statement the cooperation and collaboration are the key words that make for an effective learning situation? Discuss with examples. [Dec-2012, Q.No.-2]

Or

What are the advantages of organising pair/ groupwork in teaching? Give an example from your own teaching experience where group/ pair work was organised successfully to develop learner's skills.
[Dec-2010, Q.No.-3]

Ans. In order to become an effective teacher, besides planning of lessons, use of audio-visual aids, adopting varying techniques in the classroom, it is of paramount for teacher to manage the classroom. By 'manage', we mean to be able to deflect all the goods that we have planned effectively and systematically, with no danger of deviating or being forced to deviate from our goals. It does not mean that a teacher should not be flexible; of course, s/he has to be flexible, keeping the spirit of the class in mind. Nevertheless, it is important that s/he develop the skill of classroom management.

(1) Pair Work

Pair work is perhaps the most convenient method of promoting active participation and interaction among learners. Typically, two students sitting next to each other 'do' something together. This could range from discussing the answer to a comprehensive question to working for several minutes on a complex and well structured task. Since only two students are involved, it is not easy for either of them to switch off. So pair work is also quite effective in keeping students actively involved in learning tasks. The types of pair work are as follows:

- **Fixed Pairs:** Here, a student works with a partner who is his/her neighbour (either on the left or right) in order to complete the work assigned. In order to acquaint the students with this new way of interacting, it is best that the pairs for interaction are the same for some time. For example, if it is a questionnaire to be filled up with questions like: (a) What is your favourite sport? (b) Are you fond of green vegetables? If so, which ones, etc.; first of all A will question B and ask him/her all the questions and fill up the questionnaire, then B will ask A and fill up the questionnaire. Similarly C questions D and vice versa.
- **Flexible Pairs:** In this kind of pair work, the student does not interact with the same partner but changes partners. For example, in case, a student has to conduct interviews to get to know two or three things about each child's opinion, e.g. A goes to B and asks 'Do you like Viswanathan Anand? Have you read about him? Which other sports person do you like?' Then A will go to C, D, E and F to ask the same questions in order to collect details from each child. Now, for this kind of flexible pair work, it is essential that you judge realistically whether your classroom has sufficient space for the students to move around freely. Flexible pairing is an interesting way of handling this kind of activity so that each one can choose whom s/he wishes to interview. In case, you have the space, it will probably be simpler to let the students move around quietly but freely. Otherwise, teacher would have to take them out into a place which has more space, i.e. a sports field or the library. In a normal class where the strength is 45-50, this kind of pair work will increase the noise level. One way of tackling the noise level is to call a colleague to assist. Another way is to prepare flash cards with on them, which can be held up from time so that the children can be reminded of the noise they are making.

Pair work is useful when the teacher wants the students to interact with each other, jot down points and then write. It gives students an opportunity to use the language and also helps them to gain confidence. If the teacher is taking up comprehension question, s/he can ask pairs to discuss a question and then agree on the answer. Similarly, if s/he is given them a letter or a composition to write, s/he can ask the children to discuss the ideas together and then write independently.

Organising Pair Work: The time factor is an important consideration in organising pair work. As a subject teacher, s/he can't afford to spend a lot of time trying to move the students around so that they can work together. It is best to use the existing classroom arrangement most of the time. Ask the students to work with their neighbour and if need be, only one or two students should be moved. In case you have a class where children are seated in twos or threes, let them work that way, e.g.

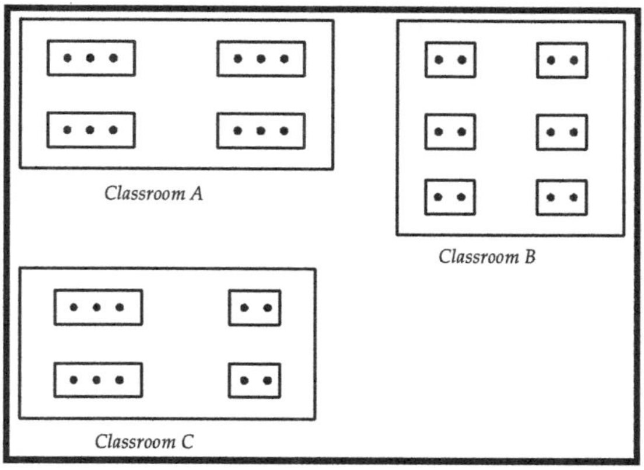

Fig.1.1

Though classroom B seems ideal for pair work, we can also easily pair work in classroom A and C. Let the students sitting in threes also work together. Here, your worry will be what will the third student do while the pair is practicing a dialogue or asking/answering a question. The third person will act as an observer or record the errors committed by the pair. This is a good preparation for group work where the students will be on their own and will have to correct one another. Some other ways of organising pair work or changing fixed pairs is by changing the partners. Often:

- The teacher can allot numbers to the students, e.g. one, two, three, etc. The class should be divided into two, therefore in a class of 40, a teacher will divide them into 20 each. So when s/he number them, s/he allot 1 to 20 and then again 1 to 20. In this way, s/he will have 20 pairs. Ask all the ones to sit together, all the twos to sit together, all the threes together and so on. Then number each desk. So pair one will sit on desk 1, pair two on desk 2, and so on. In case s/he find this too time consuming, the following method could help.
- It could also be changed the pairs by row wise. For example, All the A's of Row 1 will move to C's of Row 2 and all the C's of Row 2 move to A's of Row 1 and vice versa. This would be much quicker.

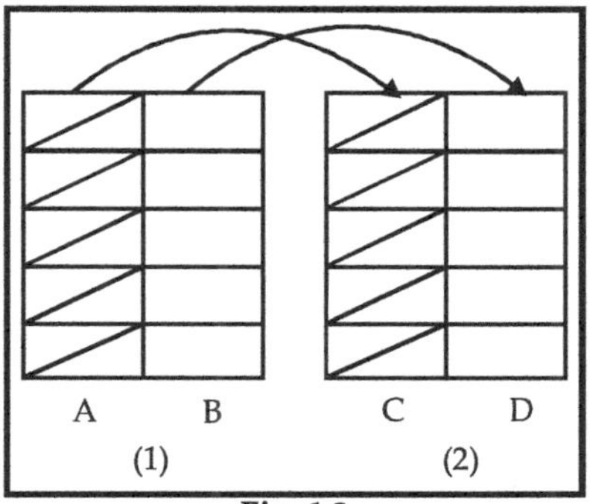

Fig. 1.2

The main reason for organising pairs in different ways is to break the monotony of fixed pairs. Sometimes, the children need to change their pairs. Flexible pairs are far more enriching as one learns much more by sharing ideas with more people. A lot depends on time and space available for organising pair work. Therefore, whichever method of changing pairs you follow, remember the most important thing is that students should get into pairs quickly without wasting time. Giving them very clear and precise instructions is necessary.

Monitoring Pair Work: In order to monitor pair work, the teacher moves from pair without disturbing the students. She offers assistance when required. She does not interrupt or hinder the progress of the activity. It is best to be a silent observer, intervening only if absolutely necessary. That is the best way to allow students to interact freely. However, if the teacher feels that some pairs are digressing too much, s/he must hover around and set them back on the right track.

(2) Group Work

Students study and learn best when they are actively involved in the process. Researchers report that, regardless of the subject matter, students working in small groups tend to learn more of what is taught and retain it longer than when the same content is presented in other instructional formats. Students who work in collaborative groups also appear more satisfied with their classes. The ability to work well in groups is one of the most important skills a teacher can teach their students, regardless of discipline. Ideally, group work draws on the discovery that comes from deliberation and the wisdom of collective experience. But assigning just a sufficient amount of work to a group doesn't mean that the students will work together. All too often, groups divide the task and meet only long enough to patch their pieces together. As an instructor, teacher is responsible for creating tasks and facilitating an environment that encourages, or necessitates authentic co-operation.

Organising Group Work: In organising group work, a lot depends on the availability of space and the nature of the furniture. In case, the classroom is crowded and the furniture is fixed or too heavy to be moved, then ask the students in alternate rows to turn and face those sitting behind them, e.g.

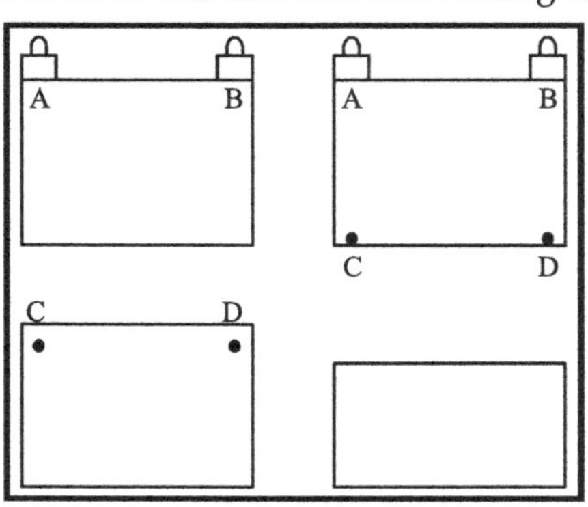

Fig. 1.3

In case, the students are sitting in threes, a similar organising of groups can be done:

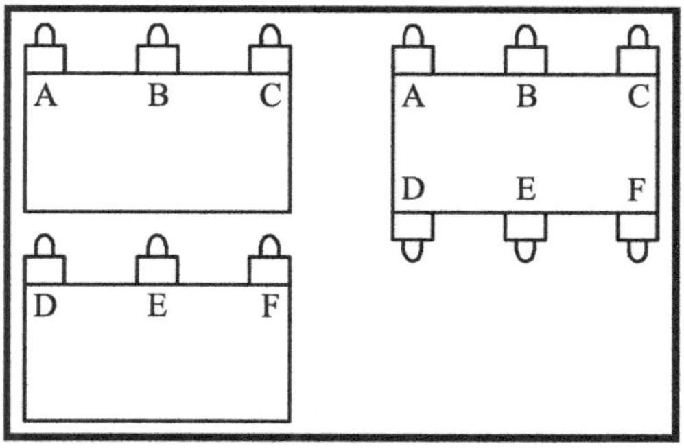

Fig. 1.4

In this illustration, s/he has to see that DEF have turned to join ABC.

The most important thing in forming the groups is to ensure that the student in a group is able to work together comfortably. You may feel that some changes are required to achieve a balance in some of the groups formed as shown above. In this case, move only a few students from their groups to others. An important aspect of group work is the means for leading or guiding – since the teacher is not there to do this. Once of the students will have to take on this responsibility. Quite often outcome of group work is the production of a 'report' that is presented (or shared with) the rest of the class. One student has to do the job of recording and reporting what the group wants to state as its opinion or suggestion. This reporter can also function as a chairperson or leader – seeing that the group focused on the given task, that the discussion does not go too far off track, that everyone gets a chance to speak, etc. If the task involves a lot of writing, one student can do the reporting, while another serves as leader. For example, if the group is preparing for a debate, the reporter notes down all the points discussed within the group, and later complies them to present it to the whole class. In the case of role-play, the reporter would need to initiate the role-play. S/he can then act as an observer or be one of the reporter notes down all the activity. The nomination of the reporter can be done by the teacher, or it can be left to the group. It is good idea to nominate the talkative (perhaps domineering) students as reporters or leaders for the first few rounds of group work. It is a way of accepting and recognising them, but at the same time requiring them to be responsible. As the term progresses, the more shy and weak students can also be cajoled into doing the job of reporting and even of leading. These small roles as part of class activities are an important training round – especially for those who are not already fluent and confident to begin with. The language curriculum should help such student develop the skill and confidence needed to be selected as monitors, prefects, captains and so on.

Mixed Ability Grouping: The main purpose of group work as we have seen is to promote interaction among learners. It is this process that really matters, not the speedy arrival at solutions or answers. For a group discussion to be interesting and worthwhile, the members should have different perspectives and opinion. Otherwise there will be very little interaction and negotiation. This is why it is a good idea to form groups of mixed ability so that both weak and good students can interact with each other. Students do assist one another because the activity requires co-operation and collaboration. We will be surprised to note the kind of peer assistance that is provided in group activities. Students help one another and correct each other mistakes too. The one thing that may be worrying one is whether the brighter or faster student might affect the progress of slower ones. Well it is true to some extent that the more able students will move ahead at their own pace and leave the weaker ones behind. However, if the group has a task that 'demands' co-operation and collaboration the weaker ones will have to be encouraged and supported; they cannot be ignored. Thus, selecting tasks that promote co-operation is an important aspect of planning group work. Putting students of the same general ability level together into the same group might seem to be the solution. The problem is that the stronger groups will finish their tasks quickly and become increasingly impatient and unsympathetic. Most often group activity leads to reports or sharing with the whole class. This should be an exciting phase of the lesson, as what 'other' groups might come up with is a mystery. All this is lost if 'strong' groups come up with 'good' reports and vice versa. The very purpose of group work will be defeated. Thus, one can see that it is highly desirable to have roughly 'equivalent' groups, each with a mixture of strong and weak students.

A special challenge that faces one in relation to group work is that of fully exploiting the diversity within the group of learners. Differences in ability are only one aspect of this diversity. Even more interesting is the variation in socio-cultural-linguistic backgrounds. Linguistic diversity is a special feature and potential feature of the typical Indian classroom. We should aim in the language class especially, to capitalise on – indeed celebrate – this richness. Choosing topics and themes that invite the expression of different attitudes and perceptions linked to different linguistic and cultural backgrounds is one way. One could, therefore, try to making the small groups mixed in this wider sense also.

Another aspect of group work that one need to pay special attention to is time. To begin with times estimate for the activity (in the lesson plan) should be realistic. Of course, if many of the groups fall behind schedule but are doing some task-related activity, which is interesting to them, s/he should allow more time. However, this relaxation should not become a habit. The follow up of group activity is important, and this should not simply get squeezed into the last few minutes of the lesson. Further, group work because it is essentially learner directed activity provides the teacher the opportunity to train students to keep to time and avoid getting sidetracked. One could build up the 'pressure' to finish on time gradually over the term. One could also appreciate the work of groups that work well in this sense, during feedback.

Monitoring of the Groups: The students themselves monitor the activities of the groups. The aim is to make them self-reliant. But, it does not mean that the teacher has no responsibility. Well, one does have a very high responsibility. One must ensure that the task one has been set is suitable and simple and that the instructions are clear. Once the students have begun working, one should get out of the way and let them function naturally. However, move around, provide guidance when asked, listen to the group discussions but as far as possible don't intervene. Provide a comfortable and a free atmosphere to facilitate their discussions. Support the group 'leader' in a group if this seems useful. But do ensure that the same student does not report or become a leader every time. See that different students get a turn in successive rounds. Don't correct mistakes immediately. Just listen and note. Discuss them and take up any re-teaching (if needed) in the next class.

Advantages of Pair/Group Work

Following are the advantages of pair/group work:

- **Students are more involved:** Pair work/group work definitely makes the students feel more involved. They have to concentrate on the task assigned. (In the traditional lecture type class, they are merely passive listeners most of the time)
- **Students provide assistance:** Pair work and group work help and encourage students to share ideas, rectify mistakes and explore meanings.
- **More language practice:** Pair work and group work give students a lot of opportunity to speak English, thus increasing the students' talking time.
- **Students feel secure:** Students who are less confident or shy do not feel any pressure or anxiety when they are working in smaller groups. In fact, the peer-assistance helps the shy ones in gaining confidence.
- **Students find the variety of tasks interesting:** The students get an opportunity to interact, discus, role-play and also simulate real life situations. All this makes the student deeply involved and interested in the variety of activities in the class.

Q4. "Many teachers hesitate to organise group work in their teaching." Why?

Or

What are the concerns about pair/group work?

Ans. Teachers hesitate to organise group work in their teaching because of the following reasons:

- **Noise level will be too high:** The noise level will definitely be higher than in a traditional class i.e. where the teacher is in full control of the class. The traditional class moves at the same pace as the teacher (or so she thinks). However, don't let the noise alarm or bother the teacher, if it doesn't disturb the nest class. The students of course, will not be bothered by the noise if they can hear one another easily. Moreover, they would be busy with the activity. But if the situation gets out of hand, teachers need to stop the activity and ask students to proceed more quietly. The message that the noise level is too high should be quite clear.
- **Large classes are a problem:** It is true that large classes requiring many students to be set up to work simultaneously can be a problem because of noise, and of the strain on the teacher while monitoring. However, it is in the large class that the opportunity for the teacher's direct personal interaction can cover only very few students. So group work should be taken up often. We should evolve ways of organising the groups (the seating arrangement) quickly and quietly. Until the skills of working together and the ability to work primarily in English have been built up, the tasks should be simple. This is necessary to reduce the monitoring load. If teachers cannot ensure that group work will proceed reasonably satisfactorily (through careful preparation, clear guidelines and adequate monitoring) it is better not to take up group work.
- **Fixed furniture:** As explained earlier, teachers don't have to move the furniture, just ask the students to turn around in order to form groups.
- **The students may not speak in English all the time:** It is only natural for the students to shift to their mother-tongue, when they get excited. However, be alert and active and move around risky. Keep the activities at the right level, so that they do not have to struggle with the language.
- **All the students may not understand instructions in English:** This is a distinct possibility and we should be prepared for it. It is essential that all students are clear about the instructions and the task before they begin the activity. So we should keep the instructions in English very simple, and also state them explanations in the regional language they know. But don't make using regional language a habit. The aim is to gradually bring the students to the point where they can follow instructions and discussion in English, and participate actively by speaking in English.
- **The best students will do all the work** while the lazy ones will sit back. This can happen in any type of classroom. But it is

reassuring to know that students definitely work harder and are more involved when there is pair work and group work. They also generally try to see that every one contributes. This is a special responsibility of the reporter or leader. If we think that a few students in a group do not contribute at all, join that group and try to draw them in - as far as possible by supporting the group leader rather than by taking over.

- **The students will make mistakes:** This is quite true, especially when they are struggling to express themselves and feel excited at the same time. But be positive. Firstly, they aren't committing mistakes all the time. Secondly, they are correcting one another. Thirdly, mistakes are the first step to learning. Moreover, teachers are there to help them and to correct their mistakes. Remember that without the opportunity to express themselves in group work they wouldn't 'show' these mistakes and so teachers would not get the useful feedback that they now can get.
- **Students expect to be taught:** It is true that students and parents do expect that the teacher actually stands in front of the class and 'teaches'. Therefore, it is important that s/he explain and justify procedures like pair work and group work and also help them see the ideology behind this more learner-centered approach/technique. If the-students understand, why a procedure is being followed, they would participate and contribute more willingly and more effectively.
- **Monitoring all the groups IS impossible:** In the traditional method too, it is not possible to monitor each and every student. In group work it would be better if teachers decide which few groups to monitor on a particular day, and which others on the following day or days. Over a period of time, they will be able to monitor all the groups and assess them too. Do not be over-ambitious, it is impossible to monitor all the groups on one day.

Q5. Explain teaching in large classes in your words with its advantages and challenges in front of it.

Ans. Most teachers have the same opinion that teaching a small group of students is easier, more enjoyable, and less time consuming than teaching a large group. Unfortunately, due to budgets, space, or lack of teachers, many ESL schools only offer large classes. In some schools, large classes may consist of up to 50 or more students. While the class may look more like a University lecture hall, the job is not to lecture. Just like teaching a small class, teachers must come up with engaging activities that keep all of their students interested and participating with the goal of improving their communication skills. While there are numerous challenges when it comes to teaching large classes, there are many coping skills and activities that they can use to make their job easier.

Advantages of Teaching Large Classes

- **High Energy:** Classes with many students may be noisy, but they are also fun and exciting.
- **Timing:** Classes go by quickly in a large class, and we will rarely catch ourselves looking at the clock. We will regularly find ourselves with extra activities that we did not complete that we can save and use in our next class.
- **Participation:** There is always someone who is willing to answer questions even if they are just guessing. Make sure to take answers from a variety of students.
- **Fillers:** Teachers have less need for fillers since core activities and lessons take longer to complete.

Challenges of Teaching Large Classes

- **Intimacy:** Remembering student's names can take a while. Teachers may feel that they do not get to know their students as well as they would like to.
- **Anxiety:** Some teachers feel anxious being so outnumbered by the students. In addition, some students are afraid to ask questions or participate in a large class.
- **Student needs:** Meeting individual needs can be difficult or impossible when class size is very large.
- **Marking:** Grading assignments and tests can be very time consuming, and our pay will generally be the same for a smaller class.
- **Distractions:** There are more distractions for teachers in large classes, such as latecomers and people chatting while we are teaching.
- **Preparation:** Making photocopies for a large class can be very time consuming. Other teachers may be bothered by how much time we spend using the photocopier.
- **Noise level:** Large classes can become out of hand when students are working in pairs or groups. At times, we may feel more like a disciplinarian than a teacher.
- **Monitoring students:** Teachers may find it difficult to keep students on task as they monitor pair and group work.
- **Space:** There is limited space in a classroom for energetic activities such as role-playing.
- **Textbooks and resources:** There may not be enough textbooks or computers available for all students.

Strategies for Coping with Large Classes

- **Use a teacher's notebook:** Attach a small notebook and pen to belt loop. Take notes while monitoring pair or group learning. Review common errors as a whole group after an activity is complete.
- **Spread out:** Find another space that class can use for energetic whole group activities. Find a lobby or spare classroom in the building that students can spread out into when they are preparing a project or performance. Take students outside if there is no indoor space available.
- **Create a participation grade:** Make homework and attendance count by doing regular checks and making it part of their final grade. Giving a daily exam tip also encourages attendance.
- **Encourage competition:** Establish a fun and competitive atmosphere within the class, by dividing the class into teams. Teacher may change the teams once in a while or leave them the same throughout a semester. Teams can win points for certain accomplishments (If noise and behaviour is a problem, students can lose points too).
- **Relax:** Find ways to relax before class so that we don't feel anxious. Never attempt to prepare a lesson in the morning, right before class. Always have a water bottle handy. Always have an extra activity on hand in case something doesn't go as we expect it to.
- **Establish trust:** Learn unique ways to remember names and do best to get to know something about each of the students. Create a seating chart on the first day and ask students to stick with it for a while. Introduce children.
- **Manage the noise:** Establish a signal that wants class to stop what they are doing and listen. This should be done from the first day, so that students become accustomed to it right away. Be careful not to use gestures or sounds that would offend anyone.
- **Reduce marking and preparation time:** Design quizzes and tests in a way so that teachers are able to reduce the amount of marking. Use peer evaluations when possible. If students submit journals, just read them and leave a short comment and/or suggestion, rather than fixing every grammar mistake. Designate a specific time when the teacher's room is slow to do most of the photocopying for the week. This will save from feeling guilty for taking up the photocopier for a long time when another teacher only has a few copies to make.

- **Enforce a late policy:** Notify students of late policy on the first day and stick to it. For example, don't let students enter their classroom after a warm-up has ended. If students miss class, make it their responsibility to catch up.
- **Share the e-mail address:** In a large class, teachers will find themselves feeling drained before and after class if they let students come early or stay late to ask questions every day. This alone can make them hate their job, especially if they are not paid for hours when they are not teaching. Encourage students to e-mail with questions, and answer them on time. If they don't like the e-mail suggestion, try finishing the class ten minutes early once in a while and allow students free conversation time. Take questions on a first come basis during this time.

Activities to use in Large Classes

- **Small group discussions:** Use topics related to a theme, or ask students to submit topic suggestions.
- **Who Am I?:** Tape the name of a famous person to the back of each student. Students go around the room asking questions and trying to identify themselves. Once they guess who they are, they can place their nametag on the front and continue helping other students to identify themselves.
- **Team spelling contests:** Each student who gets the spelling correct gets a point for their team.
- **Balderdash:** Large class can be split into teams. Teacher calls out a word and students have to write down the part of speech and definition. Each student to get both correct gets a point for her team.
- **Write the question:** Large class can be split into teams. The teacher calls out an answer and the students have to write the question. (e.g. "Lynn") Each student to write the correct question gets a point. (e.g. answer: What's your middle name?")
- **Questionnaires:** Students circulate around the room asking each other question. Students can create their own questions on a given topic or theme, or teacher can provide the questionnaire handout. Follow up by asking each student to report the most interesting answer they received.
- **Categories:** The teacher calls out a category, such as fruit, and each student has to name a fruit when it is his turn. If a student hesitates for more than five seconds, s/he has to choose a new category and sit out the rest of the game. The last person to get out wins.

Q6. What are the different roles of the teacher? Explain.

Or

Write a short note on Teacher as resource. [Dec-2010, Q.No.-1(a)]

Ans. The role of teacher in the educational set up is very important. It is a two-way process, i.e. student and teacher. It can be considered as the two sides of the same coin. It is beyond argument that teacher is a backbone of the society, country and the educational system. S/he represents whole of the society in school, which is a sub-society or mini society. The citizens of tomorrow are her/his students and the future of the country lies in the hands of the teachers. She has to understand and be able to play these roles well (at various different times) to make classroom teaching effective. Thus, teachers play an important role in different capacities. These roles of a teacher are described as follows:

- **Teacher as an organiser:** The most important role of the teacher is to be a good organiser. The students must know what they are expected to do. In case, the student doesn't understand what she's supposed to do, there would be confusion and the activity would prove to be ineffective. By 'organisation' we mean all the stages, such as instructions - demonstration (if need be), organising group work, pair work, individual work and then finally feedback to be taken from the students to see how well they've assimilated the activity. Therefore, it is absolutely necessary that the teacher develops these organising skills.
- **Teacher as a prompter:** It is often seen that the teacher sets the task well and the instructions are very clear, but the students need some initial prompting. In such a case, the teacher needs to motivate the students by initiating the activity, or making a few suggestions to set the ball rolling. For example, A student who is unable to answer the question due to shyness or confusion, a slight prompting by the teacher can prove beneficial by giving him/her the lead sentence or a clue to encourage the student to answer.
- **Teacher as a resource or consultant:** When a group task is set, the teacher has to move from group to group to see that the activity is proceeding in a desirable direction, and that the students are interacting effectively. Wherever the teacher feels that the students need help, she can offer assistance. As a consultant, she is available and offers help, but does not intervene and take control. By moving from group to group, the teacher can make an upto date and ongoing assessment as to the progress of each group.
- **Teacher as a co-communicator or fellow-participant:** The teacher may also participate in some activities such as role-play or simulation. This would help her to present new ideas informally and to assess the group for better future planning. It will help a great deal in building a better rapport with her

students. The only snag here is that the teacher may find it difficult to assume a role and keep to the level of the students (since she knows the materials and all the details such as expected answers).

Another danger is of the teacher dominating the discussions. Therefore, the teacher will have to make a conscious effort to be part of the group and role-play as a student.

- **Teacher as a controller:** The teacher plays the role of a controller when she directly controls the proceedings of the class. She decides about the work of the students, and also what and when they speak. This is most relevant at the time of the feedback session when the students are reporting their decisions or reactions, e.g. in a debate or a role-play when the group leaders stand up and read out their decisions.

The teacher as a controller is the traditional role, one which many people (students and parents) see as the proper one. This is related to the more basic notion of the teacher as authority—the one who possesses (correct) knowledge and gives this to (ignorant) students.

Q7. What are the causes for discipline problems?

Or

As a teacher, what can you do to maintain discipline in the class?

Or

Do you agree with the statement, "Many discipline problems arise due to the teacher herself"? Comment.

Or

Write a short note on Factors leading to inattentiveness in an English class. [Dec-2010, Q.No.-1(d)]

Ans. Some of the problems related to discipline that come up in class are actually caused by what the teacher does. So the teacher him/herself might be responsible for indiscipline, of course without realising it usually.

- **Don't raise your voice:** It is disastrous to try to establish control over a class by screaming or raising one's voice. The noise level of the class will also automatically rise. In fact, it has been found quite often that a quiet voice is more effective in showing the teacher's displeasure and restoring order.
- **Don't be insensitive:** A teacher should be sensitive to the needs and feelings of the students or else they will feel rejected and even loose respect for her.
- **Don't go to class unprepared:** Students are very keen and alert judges. They can quite accurately sense that the teacher isn't adequately prepared. The teacher must therefore be well prepared, and also be knowledgeable so that she can anticipate several possible questions which the students may ask her.

- **Don't let the lesson become boring:** It is important to make the class interesting so that student's interest is maintained. If the class is boring, the students are likely to misbehave.
- **Don't break the norms:** If the teacher and the class have worked out some group norms for better conduct of the class, e.g. punctuality, then the teacher should ensure that she is also punctual.
- **Don't make empty threats:** It is important not to threaten to punish a student or a group and then not do so, or forget because you are no longer angry. If 'punishment' is called for, this should be announced and carried out quickly.
- **Don't be inconsistent or partial:** The teacher must be consistent in her behaviour. If a student comes to class everyday without a book and this is ignored, it is unfair to punish him/her after a week for this. Also the same criteria for praising or scolding should be applied to all students, otherwise the very damaging impression that you have favourites will be formed in their minds.

Thus, far we have looked at how what the teacher does can lead to problems. Some other factors that lead to inattentiveness and indiscipline are as follows:

- **Physical conditions (Time and Weather):** Factors such as heat, humidity, fatigue which vary from time to time can also affect students' behaviour. It is noticed that the class is generally attentive in the morning, and the attention span seems to deteriorate towards the later part of the day. In parts of India where the summer is very hot, students find it very difficult to concentrate in the afternoons. The teacher should be sensitive to these external factors and not find fault with the students.
- **Student's attitude:** The atmosphere in class depends to some extent on the way the students view the class and the subject. Although the students in India by and large, are interested in learning English, it has been seen that in the higher classes they tend to take it lightly, laying more stress on science, commerce, math, etc. as subjects. So, teacher needs to make the English class more interesting with many surprises and challenges so that the students look forward towards it.
- **An attention-seeking device:** It has often been seen that adolescents and even young children misbehave in various ways for the sake of getting attention. A teacher can be quite prepared for this behaviour especially when she is aware that the student only has a desire to be noticed. Therefore, it's best to handle such behaviour positively by channelising it into some relevant activity in the class itself. This will meet the need for attention as well as promoting responsible behaviour on the student's part.

Q8. Write a short note on Managing Discipline Problems in the classroom.

Or

How can the teacher deal with indiscipline in the class?

Or

Write a short note on Dealing with Indisciplined Students in English Class. [June-2011, Q.No.-1(b)][June-2012, Q.No.-1(a)]

Ans. There are number of things a teacher must keep in mind when dealing with students who behave badly. There is a basic rule: s/he must see that s/he doesn't hurt them physically or emotionally. This would prove psychologically harmful to the student, and his/her purpose is surely not to harm them but to better them as individuals. Punishments, if any, should be seen as reasonable and fair, never vicious. The ability to control a group of student depends on the personality of the teacher and also the rapport that s/he develops with them. There are some tips to be kept in mind.

- **Immediate action:** If the students indulge in deviant behaviour, the teacher must take instant action and not allow it to persist for a long time, e.g. if a student is coming late to school repeatedly, the teacher should speak to the student immediately after the class.
- **Counsel after class:** One of the most effective way of tacking a student is counselling after class. A heart to heart talk, explaining the anti-social behaviour to the student and given an opportunity to him/her to explain to the teacher why s/he behaves the way s/he does, would prove beneficial in sorting out many issues. The teacher should also clearly explain the consequences of not improving.
- **Stop teaching:** Whenever the students disrupt the class, the teacher must stop teaching and tell the student who are misbehaving to stop doing so immediately. The moment the teacher stops teaching, it is clear that the teacher means business and will not tolerate misbehave in the class.
- **Talk to the parents:** In several cases, a talk with the parents will improve the behaviour of the student. It would also give a better insight into the causes/reasons for such behaviour. Parental assistance will help the teacher to understand the student and find ways of improving his/her behaviour.
- **Adapt and be sensitive:** In case, the entire class is gradually getting out of control, then it's a signal that the activity is boring; the best way of controlling them is by changing the activity, e.g. if they are reading immediately switch over to a writing task which would keep them all quiet and involved. The teacher must learn to adapt and be sensitive to the mood of the class.

- **Change seats:** If a few students are disrupting the class, change their seats. Separating the troublemakers is quite effective in controlling indiscipline.

Q9. What are the different ways in which a teacher can monitor his/her teaching? How would that benefit his/her teaching?

Or

What is the importance of monitoring in teaching?

Or

How can teachers monitor their own classroom teaching? What aspects of your own teaching-learning should you monitor as a teacher? [June-2011, Q.No.-2][Dec-2011, Q.No.-5]

Ans. Monitoring is an obtained skill, which expectantly becomes a good habit. Less experienced teachers may feel that they need to monitor closely and maintain control of activities, while other teachers feel that they should be involved at all times and that monitoring is the solution.

Ways to Monitor a class

The aspects of teaching-learning would be monitored by the teachers to examine the need of monitoring classrooms. Self-monitoring is simply the practice of teacher themselves observing and reflecting on what takes place in class with a view to bringing about desirable changes in teaching and learning.

No matter what kind of class it is, it seems to have certain factors that are common. The list of factors is likely to include factors that related to (i) different stages of teaching-learning, (ii) the main participants in the class, i.e. teacher and students, and what they bring to a class by way of their beliefs, attitudes, expectations, assumptions about teaching-learning, and (iii) the physical features of the classroom.

A teacher would have realised while doing this task that each of these factors overlaps to quite an extent with other factors. This does not matter. This fact means that a lesson is a complex combination of different factors and, is therefore, holistic. Oftenly, it is quite difficult and sometimes impossible to isolate factors and examine them individually. This does not mean that we cannot look closely at a few of the aspects at a time. We might want to look at the same phenomenon from different perspectives, i.e. from the teacher's perspective, from the perspective of students, and so on.

One can monitor his/her own class systematically in a principled way. In talking about it, have to and cover as many aspects of a class as possible. For example, teachers' and students' beliefs about language, and language learning that affect the actual learning in the classroom, the roles of teacher and students, classroom interaction which is a major factor in language learning, the nature of language learning task – including tasks used for assessment and so on. We can collect information about the different aspects of teaching and learning using a variety of different procedures. These procedures incorporate a formative element by allowing us to get continuous, on-going feedback about the class, about the different aspects of ELT curriculum in process. They seek to provide the teacher with insights into what actually happens when teaching and learning is taking place.

The main procedures are diaries (also referred to as journals and field-notes), observation, checklists, inventories and self-assessment forms.

Belief about Teaching Language

(1) The teachers' beliefs and attitudes influence the ways they behave in the classroom. Whether they are presently a teacher or not, as students, they would have seen different kinds of teachers, for example, teachers with different styles. Teachers' style is inevitably influenced by their attitudes and beliefs; for example, the nature and role of knowledge, in the case of language learning, their view of language and the nature of learning and teaching. According to the views, one holds on these and other related issues, one could be what Douglas Barnes calls a 'transmission teacher' or an 'interpretation teacher'. These two basic types are not extreme or the other. In very general terms, a transmission teacher maintains a high degree of control over the learners in order to impart knowledge, which s/he embodies. The subject matter is central and the teacher of this type will reward contributions from learners, which s/he approves of. The teacher also judges whether the learners have come up to the expectations set prior to teaching. On the other hand, an interpretation teacher prefers to disperse responsibility for learning organises classroom activities, sets up learning tasks and assists learners in doing these activities. S/he also allows for individual learning styles, and therefore, for differential learning.

(2) Teachers can analyse their own beliefs about teaching with the help of a checklist suggested below. Select 5 statements that most closely reflect beliefs about how English is learnt and how it should be taught.

- Language is a set of grammatical structures and words which are to be taught systematically in class.
- Language is meaningful communication and is learned by practice in informal situations.
- When students learning English as L2 make errors, these errors should be corrected immediately and later explained through examples.
- When students learning English (L2) make errors, it is best to ignore them as long as we know what they are saying.

- Students learning English (L2) usually need to master some of the basic listening and speaking skills before they can begin to read and write.
- It is important to repeat and practice a lot for learning a language.
- The most important part of learning a second/foreign language is learning the grammar.
- It is easier for children than adults to learn English as a second language.
- It's not necessary to actually teach students how to speak English (L2), they usually begin speaking on their own.
- Everyone can learn English.

Learners' Beliefs and Attitudes about Language Learning

Learners, too bring to learning their own beliefs, goals and attitudes which influence how they learn. We know that learning is the goal of teaching, but learning is not the mirror image of teaching. We may want to know what assumptions and expectations learners bring to classrooms. Teachers could draw up an inventory as shown below and give it to their students for their opinion. Find out from students to what extent they agree with each of these statements:

- We need to practice every day to improve our English.
- It's not correct to ask the teacher when you have a doubt.
- It's enough if the teacher gives grammar exercise(s) as homework.
- English is the most important language in the world.
- I like group work because when I make mistakes my friends correct me.
- English is much more difficult than other language.
- Teachers should explain grammar rules in the class.
- It is important to speak English very well.
- It is better if the teacher corrects all our mistakes.
- You need to know a lot of words if you want to know English.
- I know the rule but I forget it when I speak.

Tasks/Exercises in Class

Teachers might be interested in how well the tasks/exercises/activities we set up or measured up, to the criteria we had in our mind. We could list a set of criteria as suggested below and, observe and record our views as the class progresses.

Table.1.1

	At the end of 20 mts	At the end of the class
Tasks	Yes/No	Yes/No
(1) Were based on real-life needs (2) Provided opportunity for skill-practice (3) Provided for di? erent levels of learners (4) Allowed interaction among students (5) Promoted information sharing (6) Encouraged learners to re? ect critically (7) Encouraged learners to evaluate themselves (8) Were interesting/informative/challenging		

Classroom Observation as a whole

(1) If on the other hand teachers would like to monitor their class as a whole, they could use this observation schedule as:

Table 1.2: Observation Schedule [Make observation after 20 and 40 minutes]

	YES	NOT SURE	NO
(1) All instructions were clear (2) The class understood what was wanted at all times (3) Every student was involved at some point (4) Students were interested in the lesson (5) The teacher made sure all students understood (6) Materials and learning activities were appropriate (7) Class atmosphere was positive (8) The pacing of the lesson was appropriate (9) There was enough variety in the lesson (10) There was the right amount of teacher talk (11) Error correction and feedback were appropriate (12) There was genuine communication (13) Group work was well organised (14) Explanation of points of language were clear			

At the end of the class, the teachers could note down any comments they may have about each of these statements and the class as a whole. This exercise is based entirely on their own retrospective observation. Another exercise they could try is to record their class on an audio-tape recorder. Play it at the end of the class and then make comments over it.

(2) The teacher could also write a diary on the following lines to keep a record of how things were planned and implemented in class. Before the lesson, think about the plan and teacher should ask the questions in the First set to herself/himself. After the lesson, ask the questions in the Second set. At the end, answer the questions in the Third set.

First set – Before the lesson

- Is the lesson that you have planned interesting?
- Does it provide opportunities for students to be actively involved?
- What classroom arrangement will you use? What material do you need?
- Which skills will you focus on, in the classroom?
- What might the pupils learn? Write the aim of your lesson.
- Are the instructions clear?
- What provision have you made for students who finish slowly/quickly?

Second set – After the lesson

- What evidence was there that (a) the students were interested (b) the lesson was smoothly/badly organised?
- Which learners were not involved? Why?
- Write down some examples of the language that the pupils used. Was it meaningful or meaningless?
- What will you do next to follow up the lesson?
- Which of your aims were achieved? Were other things achieved instead?
- When did the pupils give their own ideas? Did you accept their idea? Did they have a fair share of time to talk or did you dominate the class?

Third set

- What have I learnt?
- How would I like to improve/change/develop my teaching in the future?

How do Students Learn in Class?

- When you need to monitor student learning, it could be done by observing them in class, working in groups or pairs or individually. Since observing the whole class may not be very easy, you might want to focus on a few students on a given day or on one group/pair on a given task. The following checklist might help:

Checklist for Informal Assessment

Dimensions of Student Behaviour **Student's Names**

Use these letters to code Performance: F= frequently O= occasionally R= rarely N= never				
1. Substantiates own views 2. Argues logically 3. Shows creativity/originality 4. Responds to other views/ideas 5. Asks relevant questions 6. Attempts to answer questions when asked 7. Obstructs discussion (monopolises, is discourteous/disruptive, etc.) 8. Uses L1 (mother tongue)				
Comments				

- If, on the other hand, teacher wants students to monitor themselves and give their views on it to him/her, s/he could give them a self-evaluation form as suggested below. This could be repeated every fortnight or month to see any progress in their learning indicated by their entries.

Checklist for Self-evaluation of Learners

(1) How much time outside class have you spent in

Speaking English? ______________________________

Listening to English? ____________________________

Reading English? ________________________________

Writing English? ________________________________

(2) Who have you spoken to this week in English? (not including your teacher) Do you feel your conversations were generally successfully?

Yes/No ☐ **Why?** ___________________________

(3) What films/TV programmes/radio programmes have seen/listened to this week?

What did you think of it?

Did it help you with your English?

If yes, how?

If no, why not?

(4) Have you written anything in English this week? If yes, what?

(5) Write down ten new words in English that you have learnt this week.

(6) Do you feel confident using these words when you speak/write?

(7) Where did you learn them?

Other context (please specify)

(8) What progress do you feel you have made in English this week?

a lot quite a lot a little not at all

Speaking...

Listening...

Reading...

Writing...

(9) What are you going to work on/try to improve next week?

Speaking...

Listening...

Reading...

Writing...

How are you going to do this?

(10) Now rate your progress for this week on your own personal scale from 1-11

(1 = lowest 11 = highest) 1 2 3 4 5 6 7 8 9 10 11

Importance of Monitoring in Teaching

However, it's not noticed that teachers monitor carefully and successfully all the time, and their teaching is therefore very relevant to the needs of their students. Far from it, in fact in all areas of education and language courses are no exception, there is the persistent problem of the curriculum-in-operation not being very effective or satisfactory. Even newly designed courses, supported by sophisticated materials and appropriate teacher orientation reveal many inadequacies, especially when followed in a variety of institution. The explanation lies in the fact that the teaching-learning process is not a simple and straightforward matter of predetermined and neatly organised inputs leading to clearly predictable outcomes. Sometimes it is observed that, even much simpler operations can go wrong. For example, when assembling a household gadget following a manual, or when baking a cake using a recipe, following a set procedure sometimes does not guarantee success.

It should not surprise us therefore, that in our teaching-learning endeavours, there is nearly always gap between our intentions and what is realised or the achievements. The processes activated in class (cognitive, motivational, interpersonal, etc.) are influenced by various factors, thus making outcomes highly unpredictable. This does not mean that we give up and accept, that teaching cannot be planned and organised and made more effective. This complexity of the teaching-learning situation presents us as individual teachers with a challenge that of monitoring several aspects of the actual situation and going as far as possible to take account of the information obtained as a lesson progresses. A plan for teacher should not be followed like a recipe, but used as a starting point for further 'situation-specific' decisions. This need for modification or adjustment of plans is pointed by flexible planning. Hence, the teacher must keep getting 'up-to-date' information (especially about the learner involvement and progress) and 'fine tune' her planned inputs accordingly. Monitoring is the means of obtaining feedback on an ongoing basis so that teaching can be made sensitive or responsive to the immediate situation in the class.

Monitoring needs to be carried out in a more conscious and systematic manner if it is to help with 'improving' instruction. Monitoring of instruction can, of course, be done by others (outsiders) as well. This has advantages and disadvantages. This process helps immediately in the (more) effective handling of given lessons. In the long-term, it plays a major role in enhancing the teacher's professional skills. The rationale for self-monitoring can be summed up as shown below:

- Very often class visited by outsiders are not feedback-oriented but are judgement-oriented. Moreover, rather than depending on external sources for information, the approach that seems to have a lot of potential for self-development is one where teachers monitor and collect information and about their teaching either individually or through collaborating with a colleague and making decisions about what alternatives to adopt. Lawrence Stenhouse, a well-known expert in curriculum-research is of the opinion that all well-founded curriculum research and development, whether the work of an individual teacher, of a school, of a group working in a teachers' centre or of a group working within the coordinating framework of a national project, is based on the study of classrooms. It, thus, rests on the work of teachers. He further adds, 'It is not enough that teacher's work should be studied: they need to study it themselves'.
- A teacher who has an awareness of teaching and its different components is better prepared to make appropriate judgements and decisions in teaching.

- Another related concept to self-monitoring is the view that experience by itself is insufficient as a basis for professional growth. For many experienced teachers, many classroom routines and strategies are applied almost automatically and do not involve a great deal of conscious thought and reflection. Experience is the starting point, but for the experience to play a productive role, it is necessary to examine such experience systematically. For this, systematic procedures are needed.
- Critical reflection can trigger a deeper understanding of teaching. Critical reflection involves examining the teachers' own experiences as a basis for decision-making and self-development. It involves asking questions about how and why things are the way they are, the value systems they represent, alternatives available, etc. Monitoring involves systematic observation and explanation of classroom processes.

Q10. What is practitioner research?

Or

What role does practitioner research play in teaching? Give an account of any experiment you may have conducted in the classroom.

Ans. Practitioner research is a kind of research carried out by the teacher himself/herself in his/her classroom or school. By conducting this research, the teachers critically loot at their own classrooms for the purpose of improving the quality of instruction. It is contrasted with the outside researcher/expert conducting an inquiry into classroom processes. It is participatory since teachers and students, the main stakeholders of the curriculum, are involved in it. Teachers are no more 'subjects' who are subjected to classroom observations or interviews by outside researchers but are an integral part of the continuous research process. Practitioner research is also situational or context-based in that it is 'grounded' in classroom realities. This means that it can take account not only of the classroom as a 'real' social setting but also of the institutional factors that have an impact on the work of the teacher. Therefore, this research allows for interpretations that stem from actual date from classroom and not from theoretical arguments alone.

It is also self-evaluative, i.e. based on the on-going evaluation of improvements achieved. Teachers can themselves decide which findings from their experimentation are useful and relevant to the given situation, which ones need to be discarded and which ones need to be repeated and more importantly, why. But even practitioner research or classroom research by teacher may sound a little daunting since it appears to involve extra work and it may seem difficult. It might be therefore, useful to look at some examples of teacher who have engaged in systematic inquiry with the purpose of understanding and improving their practice.

Q11. Discuss the need of practitioner research. [June-2012, Q.No.-1(c)]

Ans. A good teacher is always doing his best to be better. There are many ways that a teacher can adopt for his/her professional development. The most appealing is practitioner research. Practitioner research is an inquiry that is designed and conducted by a teacher to answer a question about a problem s/he is encountering in his/her place of work. It differs from other kinds of research in that it is carried out by the person concerned; that is the teacher. It is a research process that is action-oriented. The aim of practitioner research is to justify actions that are taken in the classroom in hope of improving the teaching practices. **Practitioner research** is needed for any teacher who wants to:

Understand more about teaching and learning;

- develop teaching skills and knowledge; and
- take action to improve student learning.

By doing practitioner research, a teacher is actually developing him/herself. Practitioner research is done in a series of planning, execution and evaluating the feedback of action. Therefore, a teacher have to explore in his/her knowledge about how to act to solve a classroom problem. In other words, s/he will make a quest to find out the answer.

The main aim of GPH book is to provide knowledge as well as good marks in exams.

◈◈◈

2 Activities–Listening and Reading

An Overview

The learning of a language can be accelerated to a great extent by the help of some communicative activities. Through these activities, two skills can be developed which are important in learning, understanding and teaching of English language. Both of these skills require active participation of the reader and listener, in spite of the fact that they are called receptive skills. Thus, there is a great need to for the development of these skills.

When learners comprehend, they interpret, integrate, critique, infer, analyse, connect and evaluate ideas in texts. They negotiate multiple meanings not only in their heads but in the minds of others. When comprehending, learners strive to process text beyond word-level to get to the big picture. When comprehension is successful, learners are left with a sense of satisfaction from having understood the meaning of a text.

Q1. What are listening and reading skills? What is common to both reading and listening skills?

Or

Describe the skills common to both reading and listening.

Or

Write a short note on Prediction in reading comprehension.

[Dec-2010, Q.No.-1(e)]

Ans. Listening is one of the most important parts of the oral communication. Listening is a receptive rather than a productive skill, but it is an equally important skill. Most learners spend considerable more time in listening to the foreign language than in producing it themselves. It is not only that they must understand what is said to them during face-to-face interaction; there is a vast range of situations where they will be the silent receivers of messages directed at them.

There are times when a person might find him/herself listening to something in a relaxed way, not paying attention to every word, but for the sheer pleasure of following the content of what is said. Listening to a radio programmeof songs or a cricket commentary may be for driving pleasure only – or only for relaxation, where language poses no problem. At other times, the same person might find him/herself in a situation where s/he has to listen with great attention, because s/he is trying to pick up and remember a series of important instructions as in the case of the employee listening to his/her boss's orders. Now here we have two different types of listening experiences – those in which the language level is well within the listeners capacity, and which therefore allow him/her to listen for pleasure or interest without having to make a great deal of effort and the other situations in which s/he needs to pay more attention to content and language. The first type of listening can be called 'extensive listening'. The second type of listening might be called 'intensive listening'.

The Reading Skill

Have you thought over this fact, "Why do we need to give practise to our students in reading? What do they do when they read a text?"

Reading for Understanding

Step I: Look at the passage and the sentences in the boxes below and identify which uses of the text develop the student's skill reading for understanding.

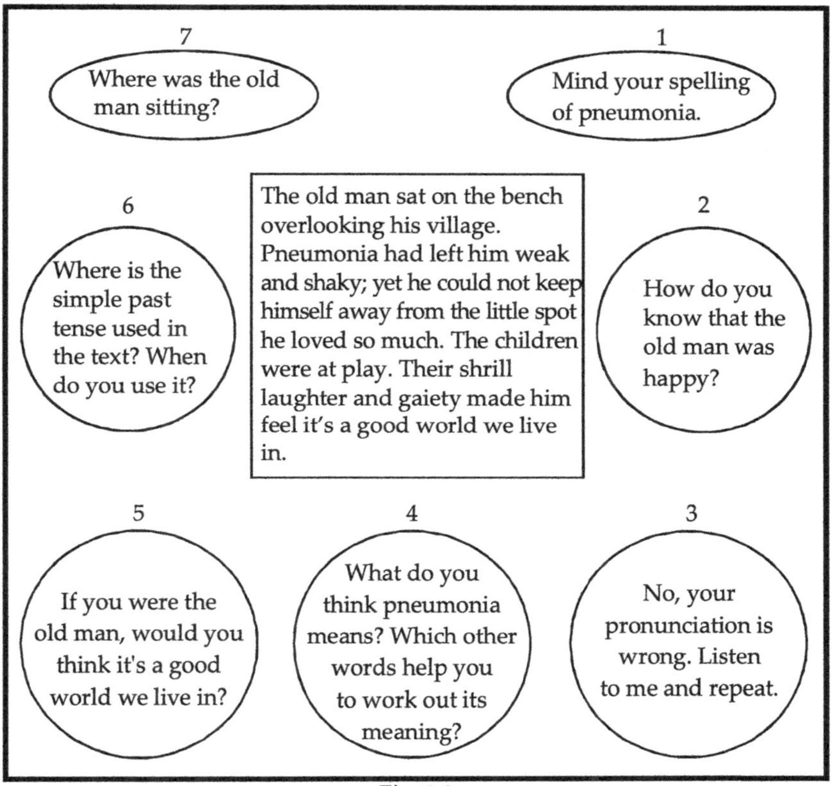

Fig. 2.1

Step II: After reading the above boxes, the teacher will find that following boxes help students in understanding the text: 2,4,5,7, (No. 4 helps students in understanding the vocabulary)

Therefore, reading is for understanding and what do we read for.

Table 2.1

For Pleasure	For work	For Survival
Letters from friends, magazines, fiction, poetry, biographies and soon.	Notices, advertisement, business letters, reports, articles, catalogues, instructions, letters, official documents, etc.	Bus and trainnotice bills, receipts, receipts, timetables, street signs, etc.

How do We Read?

Generally, there are four ways of reading. These are described briefly as follows:

(1) **Skimming:** quickly running one's eye over text to get the gist of it.

(2) **Scanning:** quickly going through a text to find a particular piece of information.

(3) **Extensive reading:** As extensive reading is for pleasure, it also usually involves reading longer texts for one's own pleasure and interest. This is an activity, which mainly involves global understanding.

(4) **Intensive reading:** It involves reading of shorter texts, to extract specific information. This is an activity which mainly involves reading for detail.

For developing these skills for reading, we have to discuss the enabling skills that can help students to develop efficient reading techniques. Here are a few skills:

- Prediction what the writer is going to talk about and interpreting it.
- Recognising words and phrases in English language.
- Using one's own knowledge of the outside world to understand the text.
- Extracting specific information for summarising or note-taking.
- Skimming to obtain the gist and recognise the organisation of idea within the text.
- Retrieving information stated in the passage.
- Finding out the relevant information from the given text or distinguishing between relevant and irrelevant information.
- Deducting the meaning and use of unknown words, ignoring unknown words/phrases that are redundant, i.e. that contributes nothing to interpretation.
- Understanding the meaning and implications of grammatical structures: e.g. tense or adverb clauses of cause, result, purpose, reference in time, etc.
- Recognising discourse markers like therefore, however, etc.
- Understanding relations with the sentence and the text, layout, use of headings, etc.

Enabling Skills which are Common to Both Reading and Listening

After discussing, what enabling skills are required for developing the skills of reading or listening, let us now look at a few skills which are common to both.

Predictive Skills: An efficient listener or reader predicts what s/he is going to hear or read, and the process of understanding the text is the process of seeing how the content of the text matches up to these predictions. First, the reader or listener will try to predict as a result of his/her expectations – and as s/he continues to listen and read, however, his/her predictions will keep on changing as more information is received from the text. It is precisely this skill, which a language learner will develop in himself/herself or a practising teacher will help to develop in him/her students.

Extracting Specific Information: Very often, the listener or reader is involved in the use of receptive skills for the sole purpose of extracting information. In other words, the reader, for example, may look at a piece of written language not in order to understand it all, but for the purpose of finding out only one or two facts. S/he may quickly read (scan) a film review only to find out the name of the stars. The listener may turn on the radio and listen to only old film songs that s/he wants to hear. In both cases, the reader/listener will disregard everything except the information that s/he is interested in. This skill when applied to reading is often called scanning and concentrates on extracting specific information.

Getting the General Picture: Readers and listeners often read or listen to something because they want to get the general picture. In other words, they want to read something and as a result of their reading have a general idea of the main point of what they have read; it is the main point that they are interested in, not the details. Indeed the skill of reading in order to get the general idea (often called skimming) presupposes the reader's ability to pick out the main points and discard what is irrelevant. The reader is able to skim rapidly over the information that is given and get the gist of the text. The skill of getting the general picture, then, is concerned with rapidly assessing the main points of a text and not paying attention to irrelevance (often redundancy) or detail. In listening, also, this skill is necessary particularly since the speakers often repeat themselves, and deviate from the main points.

Inferring Opinion and Attitude: A reader or listener often has to work out the writer's or speaker's opinions and attitudes particularly since they are not always directly stated. The experienced reader or listener will know, from various clues s/he receives while reading and listening, whether the writer or speaker approves or the topic s/he is describing is favourable or not. The ability to infer opinion and attitude is largely based on the recognition of language style and its use to achieve appropriate purposes.

Deducting Meaning from Context: Even in the mother tongue, a speaker or a reader often comes across words in written and spoken texts that do not understand. Usually, however, the fact that a word is unknown to them does not cause any particular problem. Based on the context in which the word occurs (the sentences, information and grammar that surrounds it) the reader or speaker guesses its meaning. Usually this guess is right. The point is that deduction of meaning is important for a language use who will often meet unknown words, and as a teacher, we should try to train students in this as well, to guess the meanings of unknown words. Of course, readers/listeners may not be able to deduce the meaning from the context when there are a great number of words that do not understand.

Q2. Describe the different types of listening situations one encounters in real life.

Or

Imagine situations where listening takes place, the aids and the difficulties face by the learner.

Ans. Following are the listening situations one encounters in real life:

- Exchanging news with friends, making arrangements over telephone.
- Taking part in a lesson.
- Listening to the radio news/weather forecast, sports commentary, announcements, etc.
- Eavesdropping on other people's conversation.
- Telephone conversation.
- Listening to a talk or a lecture discussing work/current problems with family or colleagues.
- Watching a film play on TV.
- Listening to recorded broadcasts/announcements at airports, stations, etc.
- Participating in a meeting, seminar or discussion.
- Receiving instructions on how to do something, get somewhere.

Analysing Different Listening Situations

In real life, we rarely come across situations, where we are merely expected to listen. More often than not, we are expected to respond after listening to someone. And our response may have to be spoken or written. For example, when discussing work/current problems with family or colleagues, we need to listen as well as to speak. We often need to plan what it to be said, and adapt out speech in such a way that we do not hurt other people. This is a very difficult and demanding process. Similarly in a situation where we listen to a talk or a lecture, we are not only required to understand what is being said, but also to select the important, relevant information, and reduce it to a form that can quickly be taken down in writing and reconstructed later on – another complex combination of skills. All these complex skills need to be dealt with in a classroom situation to equip students to deal with communication in real life.

Aids and Difficulties of a Listening Situation

Students who have English as their second or third language will face additional problems when listening, due to their limited experience of the language. Given below are some of the aids and difficulties affecting the learners of English in a particular situation.

Table. 2.2

Situation	Aids	Difficulties
•Listening to the radio •Listening to news/ weather, forecast/ sports commentary	Possibility of some background knowledge, the news, etc.	•No possibility of asking speaker for clarification •No visual clues while listening to the radio
•Listening to a talk or a lecture	•Possibility of some background knowledge or expectations •Visual clues like board work, etc. provided by speaker	•Frequently, the need to take down notes, involving selection of important information
•Listening to recorded broadcasts/announcements at airports, stations, etc.	•Visual back–up notice boards, etc. •You can ask a member of staff for help	•No possibility of asking speaker for clarification •Distorted speech
•Taking part in a lesson	•The teacher normally tries to make her/himself comprehensible •Visual clues like blackboard work, etc. provided by teacher	•The possibility of being called on to answer unexpectedly •Understanding the contribution of other students
•Evesdropping	•Motivation (curiosity)	•You start by knowing noting of what the conversation is about •You need to tune in
•Telephone conversation	•Possibility of asking for clarification	•No visual clues •Distorted speech sometimes

Q3. Comment on the information processing and inference based approaches in listening comprehension.

Ans. To explore the issue of understanding in verbal interaction, it is necessary to outline the nature of content in language and the nature of the roles of the interlocutors. Practically speaking, before we look at how people understand language, we need to know what it is, i.e. understood, who is responsible for creating this content and who is responsible for understanding it.

We have some answers to these questions. For instance, we often speak of communication as the sending and receiving of information with our image of one person 'catching' this information which another person somehow 'sends'. Or we often refer to communication as a travelling thought process with one party 'picking up signals' we transmit. Although these terms account for both content and roles of interlocutors, the actual procedures they imply are of course impossible to carry out.

Thoughts and messages obviously do not possess the **physical properties necessary** travel, nor do people literally follow, pickup or catch things in the communication process. Many of these phrases are rooted in the rationalist tradition in philosophy, the philosophy which gave rise to information processing theory. "The basic idea remained throughout that communication is seen as a potentially perfect coding – decoding process, in which speaker and hearer approach an isomorphic match of meanings "Michael Rost". Once the process of listening is understood, some useful generalisations can be drawn from it, which have some immediate implications for classroom practice.

Q4. Discuss the purpose and expectation of listening situations.

Ans. Teaching listening skills is one of the trickiest tasks for any teacher. This is because successful listening skills are acquired over time and with lots of practice. It's frustrating for students because there are no rules as in grammar teaching. Speaking and writing also have very specific exercises that can lead to improved skills. This is not to say that there are not ways of improving listening skills, however, they are difficult to quantify.

Our expectations may be linked to our purpose in listening. If we want to know the answer to a question, then we ask and expect to hear a relevant response. In many cases, this leads to our "listening out" for certain key phrases or words. When we ask a question, "Where are you going?" We, then, expect the answer in which the name of the place will be mentioned. If we listen to a lecture, we generally know what the subject is going to be. This is a close relationship between listener's expectation and purpose on one hand, and comprehension on the other. Heard discourse that corresponds closely to what the listener expects and needs to hear is more likely to be accurately perceived and understood than that which is unexpected, irrelevant or unhelpful.

Q5. Describe the interpersonal and transactional functions of language.

Ans. According to Michael Rost, communication is a potentially coding and decoding process in which the hearer and the speaker approach an isomorphic match of meaning — this matching depends upon the purpose of the listener and the speaker. There is clearly a difference in an interaction between a railway clerk and a passenger wanting to know the departure time of a certain train, and an interaction between two friends exchanging greetings and enquires about how life is treating them. In the first instance, the main concern is with obtaining or passing on concrete information; in the second instance, it is maintaining friendly social contact. Similarly, the same distinction could be made. For example, between a boss giving his instructions for the day to a group of workers, and someone recounting the events of the day to his/her friends, in order to amuse or just to fill in the silence. The first is an exchange of information or the use of language to "get things done". This is called the 'transactional function'; and the second, the use of language for establishing and maintaining social contact is called the 'interactional function of language'.

Most teaching materials in listening comprehension concentrate on helping learners cope with transactional, but it is equally important to give students the chance to recognise and use features of interactional language. While teaching listening comprehension, as a teacher, we will have to provide passages and activities, which can help students with such aspects as recognising the speakers' emotional attitude or the relationship between the speakers. Not only what is said, but the way in which it is said, is important to get a correct understanding of the social situation. Students should be helped to pay attention to such things as tone of voice, volume and speed as clues to what the speaker is thinking or feeling, as well as to the actual words used.

Q6. What are the different types of listening skills to be handled in the classroom?

Or

Write a short note on Extensive and Intensive Listening.

[June-2011, Q.No.-1(e)]

Or

Comprehension or interpretation in listening comprise processing of knowledge and information. Explain. Provide two brief examples of listening in real life where both these come into play.

[Dec-2012, Q.No.-3]

Or

Write a short note on 'Teaching Conversation Skills'.

[Dec-2011, Q.No.-1(d)]

Or

Write a short note on Extensive and intensive listening comprehension. [June-2013, Q.No.-1(d)]

Or

List different categories of listening comprehension. How would you make use of these categories in the classroom? Provide examples.

Ans. Listening skills refers that the student can attend to information in a way that allows him/her to process it. An effective listener can disregard other sounds that would interfere with comprehension. The listener is able to focus and sustain attention.

Any training in listening occurred for two reasons in the language classroom:

- To provide the student an understanding of the spoken word.

- To provide the students with a model of the spoken language for learners to imitate in oral production.

The speech of the teacher in the class, or the recorded dialogue, which precedes the drill of a new structure in the class is the most familiar type of listening work for oral reproduction. But this kind of oral imitation does not train students in listening comprehension skills because of the reasons given below:

- The variety of language forms in teaching dialogues intended as a basis for oral practice is usually limited.
- The delivery of the speaker is usually kept fairly slow and careful – an easy and suitable model for learners to imitate.
- The information contained in such dialogues is usually not very important and the learners are not asked to pay much attention to it – as the focus is the language form.

All this is very different from what learners have to face when they start dealing with real situations in their lives.

Extensive and Intensive Listening Comprehension

Sometimes a person listens to something in a relaxed way, not really concentrating on every word, but for the sheer pleasure of following the content of what is said. For example, an interesting and amusing programme over the radio which poses no particular problems of language or difficulty of concepts, and which one listens to for the sake of entertainment. At other times, the same person might find him/herself in a situation where s/he has to listen with great attention, because s/he is trying to pick up and remember a series of important instructions as in the case of a student listening to his/her teacher's instructions about some class work.

Here, we have given two different types of listening experiences; one in which the language level is well within the capacity of the students and which therefore allow them to listen with pleasure or interest without having to make a great effort to overcome linguistic difficulties; and the other in which they need to pay more attention to the content as well as the language. The first sort of experience can last quite a long time, several minutes, as in the case of easy stories read aloud by the teacher or heard on tape. In the first kind of experience, the student may not be asked to do language work on what they hear but have the satisfaction of an almost complete direct understanding of something worth hearing. This type of listening can be called 'extensive listening'. The second type of listening (i.e. instructions by the teacher) might be called 'intensive listening'. Here, some of the activities the teacher may carry out are that the students may be asked to listen to a passage with the aim of collecting and organising the information that it contains. The type of passage is usually a little different from that used for extensive listening. It contains more concrete information which may be quite densely packed and often is not easy for the students to understand on first hearing. This is because the aim is to give the students a challenge to allow them to develop listening skills or knowledge of language through the efforts they make, guided by exercises or activities related to the passage. For these reasons, passages for intensive listening should be short, not more than a few minutes long, and they should be played several times, straight through or in sections. This should be done so that students have the chance to come to grips with content. The passages need to be short so that they can be analysed within a lesson, and also because students will find it easier to handle shorter passages.

Some Categories of Listening Activities

Penny Ur suggests four broad categories of listening comprehension:

(1) Listen and make no response: There are many real life situations where students do not respond, they just listen to what is being said. In a classroom, for instance, a student is often not required to make any response. This helps the student to concentrate on the listening activity itself. Thus, "no response exercise" can be conducted and are an excellent device for exposing students to relatively large amount of spoken English. For a feedback of how much the students have understood, can be easily judged by a glance at their faces. Here are examples of situations that may be carried out by the teacher:

- **Following a written test:** Listening to text and reading it at the same time is something that is usually done in the foreign/second language classroom. The teacher read out a story and the students follow her words in their textbooks. This is a good technique for presenting new material and aiding reading.
- **Listening aided by visuals:** In this type of exercise, the students look at visual material while simultaneously following a spoken description of it. A simple, large, clear drawing can be used, put up on the board, or a number of small pictures can be distributed among the students. In either case, all that the students have to do is follow the spoken description according to its graphic representation. Classroom experience says that in such activities, students usually concentrate very well.
- **Informal teacher talk:** This kind of talk by the teacher is an excellent way of presenting listening material in the class. It can be interpolated at any stage in the lesson, serving as a relaxing break from more intensive work. It is easy to listen to, since it is 'live' and 'personal'.
- **Entertainment:** If students listen to something entertaining, they are likely to attend better and get full benefit from the listening experience. Occasionally, it is a good idea to introduce English songs and stories as some of the listening activities of an English

lesson. This improves students' motivation and the general morale and shows the more interesting aspects of the new language. Television and films based on good stories or interesting topics are very effective in teaching of the L2. Television, films, videos and audios should become an integral part of the language classroom.

(2) Listen and make short responses: In this category, the listening material consist of long sequences of colloquial speech (monologue or dialogue) broken up into short 'bits', many of which require immediate brief responses by the learners. The examples of such situation could be when the teacher gives commands; the students show comprehension by complying with them. Similarly, a teacher could give verbal instruction to draw pictures. This is an activity that is more readily done by young learners. Similarly, multiple choice exercise, true or false exercise, all come under listening where the learner has to make short response.

(3) Listening and making longer responses: Here the student has to use longer units of language (written, read or spoken) in his/her responses, and s/he has to be able not only to understand what s/he hears but also to reproduce, answer, expand or summarise as required. Thus, whereas the brief responses in the earlier instance allowed only one response in each case, those in this case are typically open-ended and the student can exercise his/her ability to produce spoken or written language. Here, as a teacher, we would like to have the feedback to find out if the students have understood the listening activity or not. The most obvious way is to ask the student, "Well, what did I say?" In fact, in the classroom three main kinds of reproduction exercises are used – repetition, paraphrase and translation – each of which may consist of either oral or written language. Another technique which is used a great deal to check comprehension is the method of question answer. The skills of summarising and note-making also help students in comprehension after they have undergone a listening activity.

(4) Listening as a basis for study and discussion: Here most exercises entail extensive discussion, and the tasks are on the whole more intellectually demanding. The listening activity may take a relatively short-time, but it serves as the basis and starting point for each exercise. Students are expected not only to understand the material that they hear, but also to be able to compare or collate its different parts or aspects, analyse, interpret, evaluate and reason from it. These kinds of activities are carried out typically through group discussions and may be summarised in essay form. There could be an activity where students hear all the information relevant to a particular problem and then set themselves to solve it, either individually or through group discussion. They may need to hear the information two or three times at first in order to master the details. They may be allowed to hear it again in the course of the solving process. This process is called 'problem solving'. Similarly, in jigsaw-listening, different groups of students listen to different but connected passages, each of which supplies some part of what they need to know. They, then, come together to exchange and pool their information, thereby reconstructing a complete picture.

Q7. Provide a leaason plan for listening skill.

Ans. Lesson Plan For A Listening Skill Class

Subject	:	English
Date	:	September 15, 2013
Topic	:	The four great singers
Period	:	IV
Class	:	II C
Duration	:	35 minutes

Specific Objectives

The students would be able to:

- know the story.
- understand the theme of the story.
- tell the sequence of the story.
- narrate the story in their own words.

Teaching Aids

Stick puppets of donkey, cat, cock, dog and charts are used. Children can be given masks of these animals to wear. This keeps the children entertained.

Previous Knowledge

Students recognise those animals and birds, the ones in the story are common to the children.

Testing of Previous Knowledge and Introduction

Questions	**Answers**
(1) (showing the mask/	It is a donkey.
Puppet/picture of donkey)	It is Nitin, madam.
What is this?	
(2) (Showing the mask/puppet/	It is a cock.
picture of cock)	Cock-a-doodle doo.
What is this?	It is a murgi.
(3) Who eat rats?	Cats.
(4) Which animal chase/trouble cats?	Dogs.

Statement of Aim

I shall tell you a story...about a donkey, cat, cock and a dog.

Fig. 2.2: Children wearing masks create interest to a lesson

Table 2.3

Teaching Point	Teaching-Learning Process		Evaluation
	Pupil-teacher's Activities	Student's Activities	
Story	Using stick puppets, P/T tells the story—Once, there was a farmer and his wife. One day, the farmer said, "Our donkey is old. Let us drive him out." After hearing this, the donkey was very sad. He thought, "My master does not love me" and he ran away from the house. P/T shows the chart or students wearing masks can enact the scene. The teacher continues the story.	Students listen carefully to the story. Students see the chart event by event. Or	Q. What did the farmer say? Q. Why does the donkey want to run away?

Contd...

Contd...

Teaching Point	Teaching-Learning Process		Evaluation
	Pupil-teacher's Activities	Student's Activities	
	The donkey met an old dog. The donkey asked him, "What is the matter? Why are you looking sad?" The dog said, "I am old now. My master does not want me now." Then the donkey said, "Same here. Come with me! We will go to Varanasi and sing together."	Students can see the masked enacting event by event.	Q. Whom did the donkey meet?
	Next, they met a cat. She was crying. She told them, "My mistress does not love me". They said, 'Come with us. We will go to Varansi and sing together."	Students listen carefully to the story.	Q. Why did the cat want to go along with them?
	On their way, they met an old cock. The cock said, "My mistress wants to kill me as I am old. So, I am running away." In the evening, they reached a		Q. What kind of a mistress did the cock have?
	forest. They saw a light on top of a hill.	The students listen to the story attentively.	Q. Where did they see a light?
	They reached the house. They saw some thieves. There was food on the table. All the animals sang together, "Bray-bray, Bow-how! Maio-miao, Cock-a-doodle-do."		

Contd...

Contd...

Teaching Point	Teaching-Learning Process		Evaluation
	Pupil-teacher's Activities	Student's Activities	
	The thieves cried, "Help!" and ran out of the house. The animals decided to stay there forever. Q. What do you think about the moral of the story? P/T asks some students to tell the story in brief.	Students recog-nise the diffe-rent sounds of animals.	Q. What did the animals sing together?
Moral of the story		Students infer the moral of the story.	
Story in short		A student narrates the story in his/her own words. (with/without help).	

Recapitulation

Arrange the following sentences in their proper order:

- There were some thieves in the house.
- The cock saw a light on the top of a hill.
- The animals were unhappy in their master's house.
- The animals' song made the thieves run away.
- They reached a forest.

Learning Extensions/Home Assignment

- Draw/stick pictures of a cat and a cock. Colour them.
- You are Moti, the dog. Write down three sentences about why you wantto run away from the master's house.

Q8. Enumerate the Phases of a Listening Lesson in a Class.

Or

Write a short note on Three Phases of a Listening Lesson.

[Dec-2010, Q.No.-1(c)]

Ans. Listening in the classes can be very boring, however, it is the most basic and necessary skill for the learner. If a teacher set the tasks out clearly step by step, the learner can be truly involved and motivated. Three phases of a listening lesson are as follows:

Pre-listening activities: Things to do before the students hear the passage, to help them get the most out of what they are going to hear. For example, the activity under the heading "The Telephone Message", where the students are shown the material on a blackboard. This prepares students to hear what is required. This is called the 'pre-listening activity'.

While-listening activities: Activities and exercises to be carried out as the students listen to the passage, to guide them as they try to grasp the main information in it.

In the activity on jigsaw-listening, the students listen to the three taped conversation in railway time-table that is given to them. This is the while-listening activity.

Post-listening activities: Things to do once the class has come to grips with the meaning and content of the passage, and is ready to look back, to reflect on some of the language points in it, or to do some extension work based on the content of the passage. Therefore, the activity mentioned after the tape scripts has been heard (in jigsaw-listening) pertains to the third phase, where students undergo the 'discussion stage'. This third phase is called the Post-listening activity.

Q9. Describe the process of reading and meaning making. Explain with the help of a reading text.

Or

Write a short note on Reading as an Interactive Process.

Or

How does a learner construct meaning from a reading text? Explain with examples.

Or

Write a short note on Silent Vs Loud reading. [June-2011, Q.No.-1(d)]

Or

"The meaning of a written text does not merely lie in it, waiting to be passively absorbed by the reader". Discuss with examples.

[Dec-2012, Q.No.-3]

Ans. To understand the process of reading, we have to know the differences between two activities:

- Reading for meaning (silent reading), and
- Reading aloud.

Think of your own experience as both a student and a teacher. In many classrooms, the reading lesson is used as an opportunity to teach pronunciation and encourage 'expression speaking', i.e. speaking with feeling and emotion. For early readers, reading aloud is of course an important aid: beginners have to discover how reading from them. But the early reading stage does not last long – normally, two or three years at the most. Do children have to read aloud after that? If they do, what are the contexts in which they may be required to do it? For most of us, once we have passed the early reading stage, reading aloud is not an activity we engage in outside the classroom, unless, of course, we are actors/actresses or newsreaders. Teachers probably use this technique with students quite a lot, but how much do they use it outside their job? And how many of their students are going to need this skill in their daily life? The purpose of reading aloud is not just to understand a text but to convey the information to someone else who has no access to it, such as reading out parts of a newspaper article to a friend, or reading a notice to other people who cannot see it clearly, or reading to someone who has lost his/her spectacles. Obviously, reading aloud involves looking at a text, understanding it, and also saying it, it is a much more difficult activity than reading silently because our attention is divided between reading and speaking. We often stumble and make mistakes when reading aloud in our own language, and reading aloud in another language is even more difficult. Moreover, it slows down the reading process and may even affect comprehension to a certain extent unless we read a text after several rehearsals.

If we think of the percentage of time usually spent on reading aloud compared with the time spent reading silently, we will realise that we should adjust the proportion of class time spent on each accordingly.

Reading for meaning, on the other hand, is the activity we normally engage in when we read books, newspapers, road signs, posters, etc. It involves looking at sentences in a text and understanding the message they convey, in other words, 'making sense of' a written text. It does not normally involve saying the words we read, not even silently inside our heads.

Now, consider a text. Read it silently on the first part and then aloud. Which technique makes it easier to understand the text? Which technique is more helpful in developing reading ability?

Another important aspect of reading is that when we read for meaning, we do not need to read every letter of every word, in each sentence. This is because we can guess much of what it says as we read it, provided the text makes sense. For example, if you are given merely a string of words that make no sense at all like this: [man jumping tiger the on lake help to] then obviously you have to show down and read every single word, as you can no longer make guesses. But try to read this sentence:

Am -- was walk ---d -- n the s ---- t, c - - r - ing a gr -- n --------

Even though more than half the letters are missing, you could probably read the sentence without difficulty, and even guess the last word without the help of any letters. We may also have noticed that as soon as we guessed the second word, it helped us to guess the whole of the first part of the sentence. This example is only an isolated sentence. If we are reading connected sentences in a text, each sentence helps us to guess what the next one will be, and so on through the whole text.

Reading is thus an active process. When we read, we do not merely sit as passive receivers of the text. We also draw on our own knowledge of the world and of the language to help us guess what the text will say next.

Look at this very simple model of the process of communication.

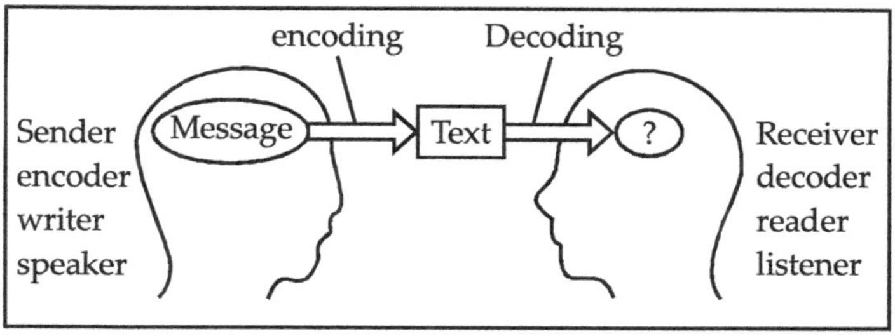

Fig. 2.3: Process of communication

On the left is the writer (or the speaker). We can use the more general term 'encoder'. The encoder has a message in his/her mind (it may be an idea, a fact, a feeling, etc.) which s/he wants to communicate to someone else. In order to make this communication possible, s/he must first put it into words: that is s/he must encode it. One it is encoded, in either written or spoken form, it becomes available as a text to any other person who reads or hears it, i.e. the person who decodes the message it contains. Once it is decoded, the message enters the mind of the 'decoder' and it is understood; communication has thus been achieved. This model is obviously too simple. Things can go wrong at any stage in the process. For instance, we cannot be sure that the decoder has received the message as it was intended by the encoder. The encoder may not have understood the language and style in which the message has been enclosed, or the encoder may not have encoded his/her message properly, in an organised manner. However, one thing is clear from this model that reading means getting out of the text as nearly as possible the message that the writer put into it. This is widely held view of reading. According to this view, the text is full of meaning conveyed through words, and the meaning can be absorbed by the reader's mind like a sponge absorbs water. To put it in another way, the reader's mind is an empty vessel into which the text pours idea, facts, etc. to be filled. Or it is like a blank state on which the text imprints the words, the ideas, etc. The writer has done all that is required for understanding his/her message and the reader need not to make any effort, but has only to let his/her mind absorb it passively. The reader's role is thus seen to be a passive on. Obviously, we know that it does not happen like this. All meaning in the text does not actually get into the reader's mind. We know from our experience of reading that text which may be easy for one person will be difficult for another.

Consider the following texts:

Text A:

Atego, quum diebus illis, itineris faciendi causa deedense provincia, Puteolos forte venissem, quum plurimi et lautissimi solent esse in iis locis: concidi paene, quum ex me quidam quoesiisset quo die romaexissem.

Many of us may have found this text difficult to understand simply because we are not familiar with the code in which it has been put; we do not know Latin, the language in which it is written. So we realise that for satisfactory communication to take place, the writer and the reader should share the same code: that is, the text must be written in the same language that both understand. But there may be other reasons for finding a text difficult.

Text B:

Behold repeatedly the precipitate progress of that triad of sightless rodents; unanimously they coursed a pace on the heels of the agriculturist's matrimonial consociate, who summarily excised their caudal appendages.

The source of difficulty here is the vocabulary, although we are familiar with the code. The message seems to be difficult because it is written in difficult language. If the message is expressed in simpler English, we will be able to understand it.

Text C:

Every living cell is a special, Frolich-style, quantum sub-class within Prigogine self-organising dissipative systems.

This text will be difficult to all those who are not familiar with the subject of biology. Even if we look up the 'unfamiliar' words in the dictionary, we would still not be able to understand the text, because we don't possess the previous knowledge that is assumed by the text.

This brings us to an important aspect of reading, namely, that the reader and the writer should share certain things in common, if they have to communicate with each other. What are the things that the writer and the reader should share? First of all, they both should share the same code; they should write and understand the same language. Not only that, their command of the language should not be too widely different. More importantly, the writer and the reader should share certain assumptions about the world around them.

Problems arise when there is a mismatch between the presuppositions of the writer and those of the reader. The writer in Text C, for example, presupposes a certain level of knowledge of the subject in the reader. The text will, therefore, not be understood by anyone who lacks this knowledge. But it is not possible for the writer and the reader to have identical experiences of life. Look at the figure below, showing presupposition and communication.

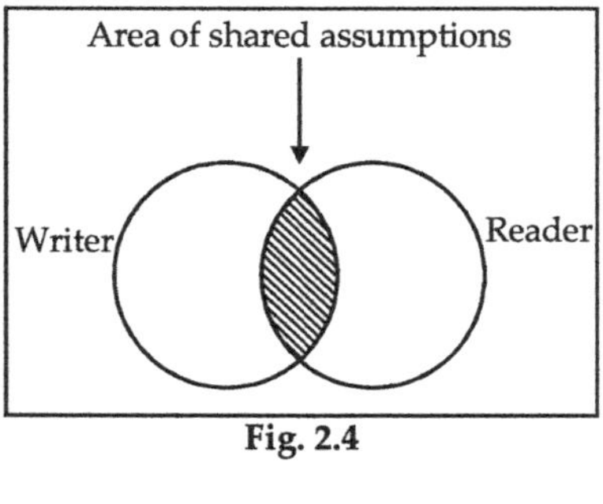

Fig. 2.4

The figure shows how two people can have certain things in common. The shaded area where the two circles overlap includes all the knowledge that they share. Including knowledge of language, it also includes attitudes, beliefs, values and assumptions that they share. The unshaded areas represent experience that is unique to each individual. It is clear, therefore, that greater the size of the shaded area, easier the communication. That is, if the writer and the reader are from closely similar backgrounds with similar attitudes, beliefs and assumptions, the reader can interpret the text with apparently no conscious effort. There is, however, the danger that a careless reader may assume that the extent of the shaded area – the common ground – is longer than it actually is. In that case, s/he is likely to misunderstand the text, trying to read into it meanings that are not there. Similarly, a writer may assume that his/her reader is likely to share a great deal of his/her knowledge, beliefs, etc. but the reader may actually struggle to make sense of the text. It should now be clear that the meaning of the text does not merely lie in it, waiting to be passively absorbed by the reader. On the contrary, the reader has to be actively involved in getting the meaning out of the text.

Good readers interact with the texts that they read. They have personal expectations about what they want to get out of a text, and they bring those expectations to bear on what they read. They actually create meanings by constructing relationships between what they read and what they already know.

In generating these meanings, they draw on their prior knowledge of and beliefs about the subject – their "world knowledge", so to speak, that relates to the subject. Readers have networks of prior understanding about a topic, what theorists call schemata. In reading, they add to those networks, filling in some of the gaps in what they know, or in their existing schemata. The prior knowledge a reader already has about a subject has as much to do with what s/he gets from a text as actual words in the text. The figure below shows the relationship among prior experiences, a text, and the meaning a reader constructs.

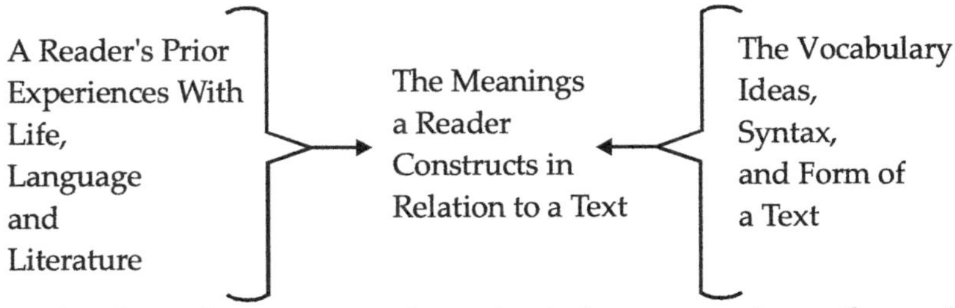

The above figure summarises what is known as schema theory. The figure also shows that, in creating meaning, good readers rely also on their prior knowledge of how language works, of how ideas are organised writing and of how different forms are structured.

Thus, schemata knowledge structures which represent a generalised knowledge about objects or events, or even about a language system, which are activated while processing a text. An important function of schemata is therefore to help readers to match what they know with what the written text tells them, i.e. to monitor their comprehension. If there is some deficiency at the level of analysing print (i.e. decoding problems like poor word recognition, the higher-level knowledge of the topic (i.e. schemata) will compensate for the deficiency.

The terms 'top-down' and 'bottom-up' are used in this context to explain the interactive process of reading. 'Top-down' processing refers to the use of predictions based on one's prior knowledge while 'bottom-up' processing refer to the role of the text in providing input through decoding, or letter and word recognition. Reading is thus, an interactive process. There is a simultaneous interaction or the reader's prior knowledge and his/her sampling of the text; to put it in more technical language, the meaning of a text is reconstructed through a constant interaction between the information obtained through bottom-up decoding and that obtained through top-down analysis.

Let us see this process at work with a simple example. Here is the beginning of a short text teachers are required to read:

(1) Keshav was on his way to school last Wednesday.

Who, do you think Keshav was? How did you arrive at this conclusion? Was it based on textual information or on your prior knowledge? Now, the next sentence of the text reads like this:

(2) He was really worried about the English lesson.

Who was Keshav? Have you now changed your view about Keshav, or not? Why?

(3) Last week he had been unable to control the class.

Are you now sure who Keshav was? Which part of the text has to be matched with kind of prior knowledge to help in the inference?

(4) It was unfair of the English teacher to leave him in charge of the class.

What further changes in your inference have you made? Why?

(5) After all, it was not a normal part of a typist's duty.

After considering these examples, we came to know that what is actually involved in reading a text.

Q10. How would you help your learners to become efficient readers? Explain with the help of a reading text.

Or

What are the characteristics of reading? What do you understand by an efficient reader? [June-2011, Q.No.-3]

Ans. The efficient of reading in the very early stages of reading instruction, teachers are generally concerned with developing the mechanical readings skills. But as soon as they know that their students have these basic skills, they should move on as quickly as possible to developing the cognitive skills in students associated with different types of reading activity. If this kind of work is begun at the elementary level, students are more likely to become efficient readers early on in their life.

(1) **Effective reading:** It also involves chunking of information that the well-developed schema makes possible. When we read, our eyes take in whole phrases at a time, which are meaningful; they do not move from word to word in a straight line, but move backwards and forwards over the text. We will understand this if we do a simple exercise. Try to cover a text with a piece of paper and read it literally word by word. Move the paper along the text, revealing only one word each time. We will find that it is almost impossible to read and understand a text in this way. We soon lose track of the meaning and we need to keep looking back across the text to take in whole sentences. Our reading slows down so much in this attempt to read only one word at a time, that we lose the sense of what we are reading.

(2) **Reading is text-based:** It seldom involves the mere decoding of individual sentences isolated from context. Look at this set of sentences:

- The mind of thinker may work in many ways. The experiments proved his/her theory of ring structure. However, water is only a solvent and not a reagent.
- There is nothing wrong in these sentences, but we cannot take sense of these sentences because they are together without any relationship among them. They do not constitute a text at all and so we cannot 'read' this set meaningfully.

(3) **Reading involves complex cognitive skills:** Readers do not merely decode the message. They make predictions and inferences- they anticipate based on what they read. They build assumptions about the overall content at the macro-level and predict what is likely to come next in the text at the micro-level. This is why reading is called "a psycholinguistic guessing game". Readers may also impose their own organisation on the information they extract from a text. At a more sophisticated level, they react to what they read, assessing the accuracy of the facts presented, the value of the opinions stated, or the quality and appropriateness of the style.

(4) **Reading is purposeful:** There is always a reason for reading. In general terms, we read either for information or pleasure. Our purpose in reading a recipe is obviously different from our purpose in going through a legal document, or in reading a

poem. But there is nothing like totally purposeless reading, even when we read a novel during travel, we read it to pass our time, and that is the purpose.

(5) **Reading speed varies according to content and purpose:** Efficient readers use the minimum number of clues in the text – semantic and syntactic – to extract the information they need. We will agree that we generally read a novel or a short story faster than we read our textbook or study material.

(6) **Reading is selective:** That is, the type of reading we do, or the way we read a text varies according to our purpose in reading. We quickly scan a page in the telephone directory to locate a name, a telephone number, or an address, but we have to pay careful attention to every word in a legal document. To put it crudely, we scan for specific information, noting only what is relevant to our purpose at the given movement and rejecting or ignoring the majority of what appears on the page because it is irrelevant to our purpose. We skim, attempting to extract the gist of a text. Or we read intensively with the aim of decoding the whole of the writer's message.

(7) **Reading is silent:** Reading aloud is a specialised skill used, for example, by actors and newsreaders, but seldom by the general reader. If it is used, its purpose is to communicate to another person a written message to which that person does not have access.

(8) **Reading is based on comprehension:** This is, understanding meaning is integral to reading rather than the result of it. The more we comprehend, the more we can, and tend to, read.

Q11. What are the common reading problems second language learners face? Provide suggestions to overcome them.

Or

What do you understand by the reading problems? How would you help learners to overcome them?

Ans. It is important to remember that learning a second language involves much more than learning the words and the sounds of a language. Communication breakdowns occur due to not only the more commonly understood syntax and pronunciation difficulties but because when we learn a language, we also learn a culture. The perceived things as right, normal and correct in one language and culture does not always "translate" into a second language correctly even when the vocabulary is understood. Communication breakdowns may occur as a result of cultural assumptions regarding age, forms of address, authority and respect, touching, eye contact and other body language, greetings, invitations and punctuality to name just a few.

Vision Loss

Sometimes, problems with vision can have an impact on a child's ability to read and interpret texts. Often it is the elementary school teacher who first recognises a possible visual problem. For instance, s/he may observe that child bends the head down to the desk or holds a book up near the eyes while reading, squints at the board, rubs the eyes, or thrusts the body forward to see. Sometime, a child may also complaint that s/he cannot see the writing on the board or complain of seeing blurred print while reading. A teacher should refer such children immediately to their parents for an eye examination. Children with problems, especially a vision loss that cannot be corrected with glasses, can be helped by:

- placing them near the board;
- giving instruction in small groups, clustered around an easel where words are written clearly in large print;
- using a reader-mate, who reads the instructions in the exercises given in the book or on the board;
- preparing special test and exercise materials in large print and dictating test questions;
- providing large-print versions of written materials.

Faulty Reading Habits

Certain faults in reading techniques have been noticed among second or foreign language learners. Many of these might have actually been acquired in L1 reading, for research shows that there is a strong transfer reading habits from one language to another. Therefore, if bad reading habits had been developed in L1, it may be useful to being to take L1 reading before developing better reading habits in the second or foreign language, at least where a similar writing system is used. Many of these early reading habits, when they continued into the later stages of reading, are known to slow down the reader and the reading process.

- **Subvocalisation:** Subvocalisation refers to forming the sounds of the words we are reading and even murmuring them aloud. With beginning readers, this offers the support of the spoken language when they try to interpret the written form. Beginners in L1 reading (and in L2 as well) are often encouraged to make use of it. But reading aloud or subvocalisation is much slower than silent reading – our eyes move faster than our tongue – so efficient readers do not subvocalise. If we subvocalise, we will tend to read word by word instead of in sense groups, which slows us down.
- **Finger Pointing:** Another faulty habit that slows down the reading process is finger pointing which children use to fix their concentration on the word they are deciphering. Finger pointing is particularly common when the writing system in the second or foreign language is not the same as the one used for L1. One way to help such children to get rid of this habit is to choose texts with large type if possible.

- **Regressions:** Another reading habit that makes reading slower is the occurrence of regressive eye movements, i.e. the eye move backwards to check previous words instead of moving steadily forward. Sometimes, even a skilled reader may have to return to earlier parts of a text and reinterpret them in the light of what has following. In this case, regression may be a sign of an active reader at work. However, children should be trained to eliminate pointless and frequent regression by practicing reading and very easy material.

Miscues Decoding Errors

Through one-to-one reading (or individual oral reading), a teacher can identify and interpret a child's miscues, or decoding errors. Miscue analysis, or the analysis or a reader's error patterns provide clues to a reader's interaction with a text. If we study the error patterns systematically, we will realise that all errors are not equally significant. Take, for example, the reading of the sentence: *'He sat on the sofa after supper'*. A child who reads it a *'He sat on the bed after supper'* has use context clues to decode sofa incorrectly. However, s/he has not distorted the meaning of the sentence in any serious way. In contrast, the child who reads the same sentence as, *'He sat on the soup after supper'* has used knowledge of the beginning consonant sounds to come up with another word that distorts meaning significantly. A teacher should therefore, raise these questions in analysing a reader's miscues:

- How well does the child use syntactic information during reading? Supposing the text says, *'The boy looked sadly to the right'* and the child reads it as, *'The boy looked slowly to the right'*, the miscue is syntactically acceptable because it is syntactically similar to the text (both the words are adverbs). But if the child reads is as *'The boy looked sound to the right'*, not only is the meaning of the sentence changed, but the miscue is syntactically unacceptable.
- How well does the child use phonic information during reading? If the child says/rid/for ride/and/fum/for fume, s/he knows the initial and final consonants and uses them appropriately, but s/he does not use the final construction to interpret the vowel correctly.
- How well does the child use semantic information during reading? If the text reads, *'The day was very warm'* and the child reads it as *'The day was quite warm'*, the miscue has not significantly changed the meaning of the text. One the other hand, if the child reads it as *'The day wasn't very warm'*, the meaning of the text has been significantly changed.

Neurological Problems

Some children have learning problems arising from neurological dysfunctioning rather than form low IQ or poor motivation. The term 'alexia' is used to refer to a reading disability that may be related to the impairment of the central nervous system, such as a lesion in a particular region of the brain. In some cases, a child with alexia cannot grasp a whole word and puts even the simplest word together by letter. In some cases, a child with alexia can recognise the meaning of words but cannot read them aloud. The teacher, uncertain about a child who manifests severe problem in reading, should consult a specialist in learning disability, because it is important to distinguish between problems caused by poor motivation and those caused by a disability such as alexia.

Q12. Discuss the types of reading.

Or

Write a short note on Silent Skills for comprehension.

Or

Write a short note on 'Intensive' and 'extensive' reading.

[Dec-2011, Q.No.-1(f)]

Ans. Reading is a complex as well as a two way process. The main goal of reading instruction is to help students develop as effective and proficient readers. According to 'F.G. French', "The teacher acts as a guide showing his class how to uncover all that there is in the subject-matter, all that there is in the words chosen by the author and all that is to be examined in the constructions, patterns and planned paragraphs in which lead to comprehension. There are mainly six types of reading:

Loud Reading: This is known as oral reading also. There is always a good deal of reading aloud carried on when teaching English. But the fact is that much of what goes under the name of reading aloud is what Ballard calls "barking at print'. W.M. Ryburn very rightly remarks, "There is very little real reading done in English. Part of difficulty is that English is a foreign language, but the chief difficulty is found in the fact that pupils are not taught to read aloud properly in their mother-tongue." At least for the first two months, no book should be introduced and consequently no oral reading should be done. During these months, sufficient practice in oral work should be given. Only when the pupils have learnt enough what they have to read in book, oral reading should be introduced. Moreover, the habit of fluency must have been developed in them.

Oral reading has following objectives:

(1) **To enable students to read with correct pronunciation, articulation, intonation, stress and rhythm:** Menon and Patel write that the objective of loud reading is, "To give practice in good pronunciation, articulation, correct intonation, right emphasis, tone, speed, etc., so that the voice may correctly interpret the sense. The words are provided, that the pupil does not have to think of the words he is going to read."

(2) **To test students' knowledge of speaking words, phrases and sentences and to give practice:** Ryburn writes test the objective

of loud reading is, "To test the pupil's knowledge of English word and phrases and whether he knows how to pronounce them, how to phrase words, how to enunciate clearly. That is, reading aloud is a test as well as a practice."

(3) **To enable students to read with expression and to understand the meaning:** Ryburn explains this objective as, "To develop reading as an art, so that pupils may learn to read aloud with proper expression and may learn to convey the feeling behind the words of their listeners."

(4) **To prepare pupils for effective silent reading:** The following are the advantages of loud reading:

- Students learn the proper method of learning, because they follow the model reading done by the teacher.
- This develops the skill of speech and giving lectures.
- The mistake related to pronunciation can be corrected.
- It trains various sensory organs, i.e. eyes, ears and mouth because, in loud reading, they work in co-ordination and more effectively.
- It makes students learn by imitation which is a natural method of learning for students.

Loud Reading has the following disadvantages:

- E.W. Manzel thinks that loud reading is not a source of pleasure.
- It does not help in penetrating the meaning. A.W. Frisby says, "The danger of too much reading aloud is that – it may lead to the written word does not convey meaning but becomes merely a symbol for the collection of sounds and is translated straight in sound."
- In later life, it is silent reading which is preferred. If a student becomes habitual to loud reading, he cannot become an extensive reader.
- It had been found that students of the class pay no need to what the other student is reading aloud.
- Only a few students are benefitted by loud reading.
- In public places like library and reading-room only silent reading is allowed.

Due to all these limitations, many scholars like P.Gurrey have out recommended loud reading are more strong. But the advantages of loud reading are more strong. So, we cannot dispense with loud reading.

Silent Reading: Silent reading is regarded as the most important type of reading. Oral reading cannot be called the best training or preparation of thought. It is often called parrot reading. A child can concentrate his attention of their meaning, only when he does not read aloud. This is why silent reading is regarded as the most important aspect of reading. It should, therefore, be encouraged as soon as children have acquired a certain amount of fluency in reading aloud. In this respect, Mehta points out, "We all read faster than we speak and children must be initiated into the silent reading habit as early as possible." Silent reading is preceded by loud reading. According to Morrison, "loud reading by students should be followed by silent reading." In fact, loud reading is latent in silent reading which is a kind of mental whispering to oneself.

Silent Reading has the following objectives:

- To enable students to read without making sounds and moving lips, so that they may not disturb others.
- To enable students to read with speed, ease and fluency.
- To make students' vocabulary expended.
- According to Ryburn, "The aims of silent reading are pleasure and profit; to be able to read for interest and to get information."

Silent Reading has the following advantages in learning English:

- It saves times because it is quick.
- It saves energy too and encourages self-learning.
- It develops the ability to read with interest.
- According to Mehta, "It acts as a deterrent against the tendency so common amongst beginners to translate what they read in English into their mother-tongue."
- In later life, it has immense value because it is used in public places and higher classes.
- It initiates self-education and deep study.
- According to Ryburn, "It enables attention and energy to be concentrated on meaning and so saves a division of attention resulting in a greater assimilation of information."

The following are demerits of silent reading:

- It is not advantageous for the beginners.
- It does not teach correct pronunciation.
- It cannot be checked if students are really reading.
- The mistakes done by students during silent reading cannot be corrected.
- Silent reading is uninteresting.
- Sometimes, students cannot understand some parts of the passage.

Intensive Reading: Intensive reading means a minute and detailed study of the prescribed prose-text. It concentrates upon language, information and the grasping of the sense. It is by intensive reading that the prose-text is taught as the middle and high stage. Intensive reading is also called detailed study.

Hence, obviously, it requires very careful teaching. It concentrates upon:

- Assimilation of language which consists of study of words, phrases and sentence structures.
- Study of sentence structure including grammar, word order and syntax.
- Grasping of the sense and
- Getting information.

The main objectives of intensive reading are as follows:

- To enable the students to understand, speak and write English correctly.
- To help them to improve and extend their knowledge and command over English.
- To give them practice in correct pronunciation, intonation, expression and modulation of voice.
- To give them opportunity to use language without fear and to develop in them the habit of thinking in English.
- To create and foster in them a taste for the study of English and to enrich their vocabulary.
- According to Jesperson, "To keep them occupied with the text repeatedly in such a way that they do not lose sight of the meaning, so that they may thus, become so familiar with it at last that they know it almost or entirely by heart, without having been directly required to commit it to memory."

It has the following advantages:

- Intensive reading increases the active vocabulary.
- It helps in learning grammar.
- It explains the meaning.
- It improves the power of expression.

Extensive Reading: Extensive reading is also known by the name of rapid reading or independent silent reading. It gives practice in reading for information only and concentrates upon subject matter. There is a little study of individual words and phrases as possible. They pass into the passive vocabulary of the pupil. Although rapid reading is supervised reading, the pupils read without the help of the teacher. They read independently to understand the information, facts and thoughts contained in a printed page.

They read quickly and understand the subject matter quickly.

It has the following advantages:

- It helps in assimilation of ideas.
- It keeps the whole class busy and active.
- It increases vocabulary.
- It has high 'transfer of learning' value, since it prepare students for library reading.
- It paves the path for individual method of study and self-education.

Supplementary Reading: Supplementary reading bears a very close resemblance of extensive reading. In supplementary reading, extensive reading is the most important thing. The function of supplementary reading is to supplement the work of intensive reading. Thus, supplementary reading is subsidiary to the intensive reading of a detailed prose lesson.

In middle and high stages, supplementary readers are recommended along with the prose-text. The number of such readers is generally one to three. The method of teaching the supplementary readers is the same as that of rapid readers.

Library Reading: Library reading is taken to supplementary reading because the function of both is to act as a subsidiary. Library reading encourages extensive reading, but there is a definite distinction between the two. Extensive reading is supervised reading because it is done in set lessons. Library reading, on the other hand, is unsupervised reading. It is a private reading indulged in for the sake of enjoyment or acquiring greater knowledge and information.

Q13. What is the main purpose of a supplementary reader in a language package?

Or

Explain the concept of supplementary reader used in teaching material.

Ans. The Supplementary Reader is seen as an integral part of the language package comprising a textbook and a workbook. Its main objective is to promote among learners the habit of reading independently. A supplementary reader is independent reading in the sense that it is not taken up page by page in the classroom. The learner reads it at home, and the teacher will check his/her reading comprehension and appreciation through questions, discussion; and, if possible, role-play.

The Supplementary Reader is like an anthology of interesting and appropriate texts - stories, plays and essays. The pieces may have elements of humour and adventure; they carry universal themes like love, fear, revenge and ambition. Each piece is followed by a set of questions as aids to understanding. There are topics for discussion of related themes/

situations and also suggested reading, listening books, stories or plays on similar themes or by the same authors.

Though no examination questions are set on it, a Supplementary Reader is an important part of language materials, and teachers must ensure its proper use and implementation. In addition to print materials, audio-video-materials are also used as part of language courses.

Many textbooks, especially those focusing on listening and speaking, carry audio cassettes with them and the reading of the book is not complete till the taped material has also been introduced. Video materials introduce variety and can promote learning by supplementing knowledge and creating additional interest in the area concerned. A happy teaching-learning situation is one that presents a combination of both print and non-print materials. This is possible only if adequate resources for the production of a variety of materials are available. In a majority of our schools, unfortunately, non-print materials are scarce. Children make do with textbooks alone. To get success in your studies, read only GPH Book.

Q14. What are the four levels of comprehension?

Ans. English as a second language is taught to make the students competent in the oral skills of listening and speaking secondly to enable them to read and write. Having begun to read, good readers operate cognitively at following four highly interrelated and over lapping levels of meaning:

Literal: Literal comprehension involves the reader in understanding the information stated directly in a text. That information may be facts and details, sequences of events, main ideas and generalisations, causes and effects. The key element in comprehension at this level is that the information is present "in black and white" in the text. The reader does not have to dig too deeply to get at it. S/he should be able to state exactly what the passage is saying, to make sure that s/he understands it. For example, if the piece of writing is about someone digging the earth, the reader should be able to state what the person is actually doing – "digging the earth". Literal comprehension is of fundamental importance. It requires a thorough understanding of paragraph, sentence and word meanings and is required for higher levels of comprehension.

Interpretive: To read at the interpretive level, on the other hand, is to read 'between the lines', to recognise ideas and information not directly stated. In doing so, the reader must make inferences. S/he may have to infer time relationships the year, time of day and season; geographical relationships, cause and effect relationships; the ages, feelings and familial relationships of characters; main ideas and generalisation if these are not stated explicitly in the text. In other words, the reader must study the facts given in the text and put two together in making the inference. Writers do not always state facts directly. They imply emotions and attitudes, and suggest points of view. For instance, an author may not state directly that a particular character is bad, but the words s/he uses to describe that person and the situation s/he presents him/her in, may convey the author's attitude towards that character. A perceptive reader should be able to recognise this attitude. S/he must be able to get beyond the surface meanings of words and see what the implications of such words are. For instance, the same persons could be called "terrorists" or "freedom fighters" according to the writer's attitude towards them. Similarly, in describing someone eating, a writer may use the words, "wolfed down", "guzzled", or "slobbered". If the writer is describing a baby eating, these words may be merely a statement of fact, but if they are about an adult, there may well be a suggestion of distaste towards the person who is eating.

Interpretive reading also involves ferreting out meaning expressed through literary allusions, idiomatic expressions and figures of speech. The writer who writes of a character, "He had no heart", does not mean this literally but is relying on an idiom to communicate meaning. Another author who describes a person as having a Midas touch is communicating something special, something meaningful, only to the reader who recognises the allusion to the king who wanted everything he touched to turn to gold. The poet who speaks of "crossing a sand bar" is referring metaphorically to death; he is not speaking literally of crossing a sand bar. The scientist who refers to the earth as a lifeboat to explain relationships aboard a plant troubled by the problems of limited resources and increasing population is also relying on metaphor to put his/her message across. One of the most difficult interpretations a reader must make is in terms of these kinds of inferences. The reader must bring to bear his/her previous experiences with language, literature and life in constructing meanings.

Critical: Critical reading requires making judgements with regard to a text. The reader may judge the accuracy of facts, the validity of conclusions drawn, or the effectiveness of the author's style. The reader may not like the way the author has begun a piece of writing, sentences together and used language. For instance, a writer may use very flowery language to create an atmosphere, or s/he may write 'tongue in cheek'.

Critical reading also requires giving reasons for the judgement and stating the criteria used in making it, commenting on the views expressed in the passage and the appropriateness and effectiveness of the treatment of those ideas.

Creative: Creative reading calls for the generation of new ideas, insights, applications and approaches. It requires invention, prediction and use of the imagination. Proposing an alternative conclusion or generalisation based on a reading text and suggesting related examples are exercises in creative reading. Composing orally, drawing and writing stories with the same pattern or same words as in those that one has read are also exercises in creative reading.

A major problem often noticed in the questions that teachers ask as a part of reading instruction is the predominance of questions at the literal level. No doubt children must "get the facts straight" before making valid inferences and judgements based on them, but the neglect of questions at the other levels may mean that children do not develop these abilities to the extent that they should. As a teacher, we should ask ourselves whether we are giving adequate attention to all the four levels, and also whether the comprehension exercises in the texts prescribed for study do contain questions at all the four levels.

The skills and strategies of reading we hope to develop in our students may be stated broadly as follows:

- **Skills involving flexibility of technique:** Variations in reading rate, skimming, scanning, study reading, etc.
- **Skill of using not-textual information:** That is information, i.e. strictly not part of the text itself: reference apparatus, graphic conventions, illustrations and diagrams.
- **Word-attack skill:** Recognising the letters of the alphabet and reading groups of letters as words, understanding the meaning of words by using morphology, contextual clues or a dictionary,
- **Text-attack skills:** Interpreting the text as a whole using all the clues available including cohesion and rhetorical structure.

Of these, the text-attack skills are perhaps the most complex in the reading process. To develop these skills, we need to use texts which exhibit the characteristics of a true discourse, i.e. texts which have a recognisable content, and are coherent and structured.

Q15. What do you understand by flexibility of technique?

Ans. One of the main characteristics of a good reader is that s/he varies the speed of his/her reading according to the nature of text s/he is reading and his/her purpose in reading it. Not only the speed of reading, but even the way s/he reads a text will vary. Student may read for pure recreation and enjoyment, or they may read to study. They may find pleasure in study type reading too, but their attitude, approach and technique will be different. They may read to find the answer to a question or the solution to a problem, to learn the main idea of a selection or some specific types of information, to discover the result of a series of events or to follow directions in making a doll, a model aeroplane, or baking a cake, or learning the legal implications of an action. For all of these purposes, they employ different methods in their reading. For example, they cannot afford to go through a legal document in precisely the same way as they read a bestseller on a journey. If they do so, they may misinterpret the document or may not fully appreciate its legal provisions.

Many students are used to plodding through all types of text precisely in much the same way, namely word by word. So, we must make them understand the need for flexibility in speed and technique of reading. In particular, we must distinguish the technique of skimming and scanning. By 'skimming', we mean that skimming over the surface of a piece of writing, or glancing rapidly through a text, to find out its general content, central ideal(s), or gist. We do this, for example, when we want to find out whether a certain article is relevant to our own area of study or research, or when we glance over a page of a newspaper to see if there is anything worth reading in detail, or when we leave through a book to find out its subject matter. By 'scanning', on the other hand, we mean darting over much of a text to search for a specific item or piece of information that we wish to discover. This skill, therefore also involves the ability to reject or pass over irrelevant information. It is the kind of reading we do when, for example, we read through a biographical account to find out the date on which a certain event happened, or when we go through the table of contents in a book to see whether a certain aspect of a problem has been dealt within the book, or when we glance through the telephone directory looking for a person's telephone number.

In both these techniques, the reader passes his/her eyes over the text so that they permit him/her to take in only the beginnings and ends of paragraphs, chapter headings and sub headings, and so on. They enable a reader to focus selectively on parts of a text that are worth spending time on.

Q16. Specify the objectives of a programme for the development of reading skills.

Ans. The general objectives of a reading programme for the development of reading skills are as follows:

To enable students: The teacher can only try to promote the reading ability in the student because reading is a private activity. In the reading class, therefore, it is what the student does, not what the teacher does, that counts.

To read without help: We cannot expect the teacher to help with the reading tasks they undertake in real life outside the classroom. Therefore, students have to develop the ability to read on their own. The teacher should gradually 'disappear' from the class – should make his/her own help unnecessary to the students.

Unfamiliar texts: An independent reader must be able to tackle texts s/he has never seen before, and the teacher should equip the students to do so.

Authentic texts: The reading skill will be of some practical use only if it enables students to read texts they actually require for some authentic purpose, or texts they will have occasion to read after they have left the course.

Appropriate speed: A flexible speed is the mark of a competent reader. So we need to train our students to use different reading rates for different purposes, instead of plodding through every text at the same careful speed.

Silently: People seldom need to read aloud in real life. All readers need the skill of reading silently, which increases one's understanding of a text.

With adequate understanding: We need to understand enough of the text to suit our purpose, and we frequently do not need to read or understand every word. Student must recognise the need for such flexibility in understanding too.

Q17. Describe the various criteria to be used in selecting materials for intensive and extensive reading.

Ans. To develop reading skills and abilities in students, there is a need to know what kinds of texts will be suitable for this purpose. Linguistic, difficulty is a combination of structural and lexical (i.e. vocabulary) difficulty. A likely cause of structural difficulty beyond the elementary levels is the length and complexity of sentences, which can make the relationship among the various parts of a text difficult for the reader to sort out. At the lexical level, if we choose texts with a high proportion of new vocabulary items (words and idioms or compound phrases), it will defeat the aims of the reading programme except when we only want the students to get the gist of a text. However, readability is not only a matter of grammatical complexity and lexical difficulty. It also depends on the interest of the reader in the text. A text that grips the readers will carry his/her along in spite of its linguistic difficulty. The opposite is also true; dull material, even if it is written in a simple language, will make readers plod along and will not help in developing their reading competence.

Intensive reading

Outside the classroom, in our daily life, we mostly read things we are really interested in, for some reason or other. The same principle should be applied in our choice of reading materials for our students. That is, we should select topics that would appeal to them and have some relevance for them. Therefore, one of the criteria for text selection would be the students' interest, which we can find out through a survey of the students' reading tastes. In addition to ensuring that the topics dealt with in the passages for intensive reading would appeal to the students, we should select texts that would introduce the students to new and relevant ideas and make them think about them, help them to understand the way people with different backgrounds, problems or attitudes feel or think, and make them want to read for themselves.

Another criterion for text selection would be authenticity of language. Authentic language is the language from which the features of real language have not been filtered out for language teaching purposes; that is, language written originally for communication in a non-teaching context. To learn to read properly, the student must, early on, learn to deal with all the features of written English in authentic real life communicative contexts. One objection that is often raised against the use of authentic language in the classroom is that it would be far too difficult for students to cope with because it is unedited and not written specially for language teaching purposes, with proper selection and grading of structures and vocabulary; that is, there is no control exercised by teacher over the language employed in such texts. But authentic language need not necessarily be difficult for the students. We can easily find many pieces of authentic language use, such as signboards, road signs, leaflets, brochures, announcement notices, advertisements, newspaper and magazine/articles, and so on which are written in simple language – not simplified language. Even if some of these texts are complex in language use, easy tasks may be set on them so that the texts become accessible to even elementary level students.

Yet another criterion for text selection is variety of formats, and organisational patterns. Outside the language classroom, we may read newspapers, magazine articles, cartoon strips, letters, instructions, cookery books, tourist brochures and maps, pamphlets, menus, time-tables, detective stories, etc. The full range of text materials must be brought into the classroom for language work. We have to choose texts from many sources to give our students a wide range of materials, in particular, texts of the kind the students will later read for themselves, for study or other specific purpose as well as for pleasure.

Furthermore, for intensive reading, we need to choose material that is not only interesting and appealing to students but worth spending time on, that is, it should be exploitable, short text are usually chosen for intensive study. A text that cannot be exploited to develop our students' competence as readers is of no use for teaching even if the students enjoy reading it. When we choose, a text therefore, we need to be clear about the interpretive abilities it demands and the methods we will be able to use to help students to develop those abilities. Students should also be able in interact with the texts on their own, without too much mediation by the teacher.

Extensive Reading

The aim of an extensive reading progamme is to establish the habit of reading among students. It is not difficult to create this habit if the books are well chosen. When we choose books for extensive reading, the criteria of readability (i.e. suiting the linguistic level of the reader) and suitability of content are even more important that when we choose a text for intensive reading, because we expect the student to read the books on his/her own. Extensive reading materials should, therefore, be:

- **Appealing:** The book will be appealing if it is attractive in appearance, well-printed and with good coloured illustrations– more illustrations and bigger print for more elementary students. The books should not be small and these must provide notes and questions.
- **Short:** The length of the book must not be daunting. Elementary level students need short books that they can finish quickly

without a sense of strain and without getting bored.

- **Varied:** There must be a wide choice of books to suit the varying needs and wants of the students in terms of content, language, and intellectual and emotional maturity.
- **Easy:** The language must be easier than that found in the course book because the guidance of the teacher or the task is absent for the student. To develop fluent reading, it is far more useful to read a lot of easy materials than a few difficult ones.

Q18. Evaluate some types of classroom activities to develop reading competence.

Ans. Reading is a compound cognitive process of decoding symbols for the intention of deriving meaning (reading comprehension) and/or constructing meaning. It involves looking at sentences and words, recognising them, and understanding them. It is a process of making sense of written language. The main way in which students learn is by reading. So, the more guided practice students have in 'making sense' of written messages, the better they will be able to do it.

Teaching Basic Reading

At the very earliest stages of learning to read, children must learn to distinguish among visual symbols (for example, the d and b) and acquire a 'sight word' vocabulary, a repertoire of words that they recognise and find meaningful on sight without a complicated analysis. This will help young children to gain control over the written symbols of language so that they can understand texts later. Therefore, it will be useful to give children practice in recognising words. A simple way of doing this is to write words or phrases on pieces of paper or cards. These cards may be called 'word cards'.

a chair	a book	a table	a desk

Hold up the first card. Point to it and say the words. Ask the class to repeat once or twice. Then do the same with the other cards. Hold up the cards again, this time in a different order. Do not say anything but pause for a while to give the whole class a chance to look at the words. Ask one of the children to say what they are.

This technique is called 'Look and Say', because children look at the words and then say what they are. But the important part of the activity is looking and understanding. Saying the words is not an essential part of reading; it is just a way of checking whether the children can recognise the words. Therefore, we do not need to ask children to keep repeating the words – the activity should focus on reading, not on speaking. Teacher can create a classroom environment in which children are immersed in meaning-filled print. Children's desks may be labelled with their names, the door may be labelled DOOR, and windows, chairs and walls may also bear labeling cards. Number words may be hung from the ceiling next to the numbers themselves and colour words next to colour samples. As children and teacher talk together, they can refer to the labels. Children will locate words and labels that apply to what they are talking about. They use the words that fill the classroom as they narrate stories or write on their own.

Furthermore, think of the early experience of children with print at home: the label on the soap they use or the shampoo bottle—the recipe for making noodles or the advertisements on TV; outside home: the neon sings in the street or the words like PUSH, PULL, ENTER, EXIST, IN and OUT in shops or cinema houses, often accompanied by visual clues. These are not constructed specifically for teaching reading, but they are part of the child's world. The child learns of their purpose as well as meaning without learning them formally in the classroom. The teacher should exploit these experiences too in the classroom in creative ways.

Word Cards can also be used to give practice in reading whole sentences. For this kind of activity, you will need two sets of Word Cards shown below:

Set 1	**Set 2**
Put your book	on the floor
Put your pen	in your bag
Put your hand	on your head

Hold up one card from Set 1 and one card from Set 2. Read the complete sentence, pointing to the words. For example, "Look, it says, 'put-your-book-on-the-floor.' Ask the class to do what it says. Show the other cards in the same way. Now hold the cards up again, in different combinations. This time, do not say anything, but give all the students a chance to read the cards silently and do what they say. The aim of this activity is the same as that of 'Look and Say' – children have to look at words, this time in sentences, and understand what they mean. The use of words cards makes it easy to change different parts of the sentence and so make different combination. Instead of holding the cards ourselves, we can also ask two or three students to come to the front of the class and hold them so that we are free to point to the message on the word cards.

Beside these activities, there are many other ways of checking the children's understanding and giving them a reason to read. For example, we can ask them to match sentence with pictures, match halves of sentence together, or drew pictures from sentences. These are simple reading tasks. We can also teach the decoding skill using class reader or a big book. One was is to put flaps over some words or parts of words and ask children to guess what is beneath the flaps. The children naturally use the context to derive meaning from print. They predict and test their predictions by asking themselves if the words they have guessed make sense in context. Another way is to prepare word and sentence cards to accompany the text of the book. Children match the cards with words and sentence in the text. The teacher can also prepare a cut-up sentence version of the text – we can cut apart key story sentence to highlight chunks of meaning or the natural phrasing units (i.e. sense groups) people use in speaking. Children reconstruct the story based on their understanding of sing, sound and meaning.

Besides, reading sentences help children to recognise words, because they can guess them from the context. So, it is useful to give children practice in reading and understanding complete sentences even at the early stages. Giving students sentences to look at and understand, not merely words, will give them more useful practice in reading than asking them to repeat written sentences aloud over and over again or getting them to 'spell out' words.

When we read our own language, we do not need to distinguish every single letter, if we did, we would only be able to read very slowly. When we read fluently, we do not even read word by word – our eyes move rapidly across whole sentence. However, when children begin to read an unfamiliar scrip, they may feel that they need to look at individual letters and try to 'match' the words with the way it sounds. However, in English this is quite difficult because the relationship between sound and spelling is very complex. For example, by, buy, light, lie and island, all have the same sound but different spellings. Similarly, the letter 'e' has a different sound in father, yet, be and pale. We cannot possibly teach all these relationships – even for the commonest words there are several rules – and we do not need to teach them. Children can gradually become aware of the relationships as they read. Nevertheless, children can profit from some attention to the ways speech sounds are represented on paper, and the teacher can help them by drawing attention to sound-spelling relationship from time to time.

Thus, in the very early stages, teachers are concerned necessarily with developing the mechanical reading skills such as the recognition of letters and words in print. However, the teacher should move on as quickly as possible to practicing the different types of reading activity and to developing the cognitive skills associated with those activities. The earlier the students begin this kind of work even at the elementary level, the more efficient readers they are likely to become soon. For this purpose, texts of different kinds can be used in the classroom.

Using a Text

The most important thing about using a text for developing reading skill is to decide what we expect the student to be able to do with the text. We read most efficiently when we either need to or want to read. In the real world, the need is created naturally by circumstances. In the more artificial situation of the classroom, however, the teacher has to create specific needs for specific purposes.

General Guidelines

- One way of creating the need to read a text is to relate the reading to the performance of another task such as note-making or information transfer.

- To help focus attention and to give students a purpose, give out questions (we may write them on the board) which students have to answer when they are exposed to the text. Remember to make sure that these questions serve the intended purpose.
- We can create motivation by working on one section of a text before revealing the next. We can ask students what they think the writer is likely to say in the next section, what will happen next, etc.
- Even if our comprehension questions are properly structured, it will be a dull activity for the students if we simply read through them from a lesson plan. We need to be sensitive and flexible enough to change direction – to skip a few questions if we find they are not necessary, or think of a few additional or supplementary questions with weaker learners.
- Comprehension question should be organised and serve a clearly thought out purpose – they should not be asked at random. We should ask 'gist' question before we ask *detail* questions, *easy* before *difficult, factual* before *inferential* or *evaluative,* and questions requiring short answers before those requiring long answers. But mix them up and vary the types.
- Very often teacher ask questions after a text only to determine how far the students have understood it. It is worth focusing attention on improving the skill itself through questions which lead students towards the main ideas of the text by forcing them to go back to the text frequently and search for meaning. In this process, students are constantly pressed to substantiate their answer with evidence from the text.
- It is good to vary the classroom activities and the types of questions asked according to: *(i)* the aim of the lesson, *(ii)* the stage of the lesson and the level or type of understanding teachers expect, and *(iii)* the capability of their students at any given point. Sometimes, teachers may even try to make the students frame question. Try to deal with different sections of a text in different ways.
- Although teachers may occasionally read the text aloud or get a few students to do it, they must provide ample opportunities to the students for silent reading. Training in reading aloud may be given only after the students have sufficiently understood the text.
- As far as possible, students must be encouraged to guess the meaning of unfamiliar words and expression from the context. This will help them to acquire vocabulary in a meaningful way. At the primary level, visual clues such as pictures could be

provided to help in this process. A glossary, if it is provided, should be selective and include only those words and expressions for which no help is available in the text for students to arrive at their meaning.

- If teachers have to handle a long text in the class, try to deal with it in several short sections. Students generally shy away from a long text ever if it is not difficult. By handling a text in sections, teachers can ensure a more thorough understanding. This is because, when the first section has been understood, it helps the student to interpret the second, and so on. In this way, interpretation of later sections builds on the understanding of the earlier sections. Besides, it is easier to hold the students' interest in a short section and work thoroughly than on a long text. Teachers can also vary their approach with different sections, thus providing for variety in classroom activities.
- A test can be used as a source of several follow-up activities. Consider whether it could provide the basis for a role-play, a discussion, a debate, or some useful written work. Teachers can put questions of evaluation (of ideas, arguments, bias, character, significance of the title, etc.) and personal response (agree/disagree, like/dislike, etc. – why?), and help the students to relate the content of the text to their own experience or knowledge. Teachers also make them reconsider the hypotheses they had made about the text in the early stages.

Introducing the Text

Many teachers feel that they must introduce every text elaborately (often through a paraphrase in the vernacular language) before allowing the students to start work on it. While an introduction can certainly be helpful, it may not always be necessary. The purpose of the introduction is to get the students interested in reading the particular text and guiding them in the right direction.

An introduction will not serve the purpose and will be a waste of time if it is:

- is too long;
- gives away too much of the content of the text;
- is irrelevant, there by confusing the students by raising misleading expectation about the text, or
- is a monologue by the teacher without any student involvement.

A good introduction, therefore,

(a) is usually short, (b) does not tell the students anything that they can find out for themselves by reading the text, (c) makes the student want to read the text, (d) help the students to relate the text to their own interests, experiences and aims, and (e) involves the students actively by means of questioning.

This can be done in two ways:

- By giving a few questions for students to think about as they read and discuss the answers afterward–these are called 'guiding question' or 'signpost questions'.
- By organising an activity before students read a text, which arouses their interest in the topic and makes them want to read. Such activities are called 'pre-reading activities' or 'pre-reading tasks'.

Examples of pre-reading activities:

- You are going to read about an earthquake. What would you like to know about the earthquake? Write down at least five questions, which you hope the text will answer.
- You are going to read about an earthquake. Try to imagine what the text will tell you about: buildings, people, boats, trains, hills around the city, etc.
- You are going to read a text about an earthquake. Here are some words and phrases from the text. Can you guess how they are used in the text? Tremors, the Richter scale, massive shocks, huge wave, etc.
- You are going to read a text about an earthquake. Have you seen or read about an earthquake? Was there an earthquake in India in recent time? What do you know about it?

Suggested Activities

A few examples of activities or tasks are given below. A teacher may think of many more creative ways of developing the various reading abilities in his/her students.

(1) Skimming for Gist

- Stating the main idea of a selection or finding the sentence that gives the main idea.
- Reading through a text and then selecting a suitable title from among three or four titles suggested, or from a list of sentences, one that expresses the main idea of the text.
- Reading through a passage and then suggesting a suitable title for it.
- Matching different text titles to a series of short texts within a given time limit.
- Matching different topic phrases or sentences to a series of short paragraphs in a given passage.

(2) Scanning for Specific Information

- Scanning a passage and underlining or circling the required information in a given time limit.
- Going through a set of pre-reading question focusing on specific information and scanning the passage for such information.

(3) Making Predictions

The activities are not only useful in developing students' predictive abilities, but also in stimulating their interest in the reading text.

- Making hypotheses or predictions about what the text is likely to deal with, based on the title alone or the title of the book from which the texts taken.
- Discussing the topic of the text or lesson beforehand, based on previous knowledge and experience.
- Indicating which of a series of question listed by the teacher are likely to be answered in a given selection and then checking the responses after reading the selection.
- Stating question the student would expect to find answered in a given selection and then checking to find the answers during or after reading the selection.
- After reading a section of the text anticipating or predicting what is likely to happen next.
- Making up possible endings for stories.

(4) Reading for Detail

- Indication which of a series of ideals listed are brought out in a given selection.
- Indication which of a series of details support the main idea of a selection.
- Completing sentence with relevant details from the reading text.
- Matching a series of details with a list of main ideas.
- Showing throughout linking the relationship between details and the main points.
- Indication which details belong and which do not, in and outline that has been made on a selection.
- Preparing charts, tables, graphs, etc. based on the material read.
- Deciding which details are important in terms of a stated purpose.
- Making a list of details that occur in a story as preparation for dramatising the story.

(5) Understanding the Organisation of a Text

- Putting the jumbled paragraphs of a reading text in the correct order – before they can sequence them correctly, students have to understand and what is happening in the text. *Variation*: Giving each student a different paragraph and asking him/her to find out, through discussion, what the other in his/her group have and sequence the paragraphs.

- Deciding which of several summaries are the best summaries in a selection.
- Discussing the function of particular paragraphs.
- Dividing a long text into two or three sections which reflect the organisation of the text.
- Making notes on the text-filling in main topics and sub-topics of a selection in a framework suggested; placing sub-topics given in a mixed-up order under a list of main topics specified; making an outline of points in a selection on one's own.
- "Jigsaw texts": giving individual students or groups of students slightly different texts concerning single events so that they have to exchange information with each other before some final task can be completed.

(6) Understanding the Relationship between Sentences, Clauses and Phrases

- Reading jumbled sentence or parts of scrambled sentences.
- Sorting out jumbled sentences from two stories and rearranging the sentences in each story in the right sequence.
- Indicating which sentences in a series mean almost the same as the sentences specified.
- Listing the sentences in a selection that helps prove a given point.
- Interpreting the meaning of conjunctions or cohesive linkers, pronouns and prepositions as they are used in a text.
- Establishing the relation in meaning among the parts of a sentence.
- Studying the relationship of sentences within a paragraph.

(7) Information transfer

For the purposes of illustration, some activity types are suggested below, which imply a range of techniques for developing the reading skills at the elementary level. Consider the tabular information given below:

Table 2.4

Name	Windows	Rooms	Trees	Gate	Door	Roof
Shivam	1	2	1	green	red	red
Bhavna	1	1	1	green	green	red
Harsha	1	1	2	green	green	green
James	2	2	2	red	green	green
Mannu	2	1	1	red	red	green
Sagar	2	1	1	red	red	red

From this, student can write six short paragraphs, each paragraph containing slightly different information.

Example: James's house has two windows and two rooms. It has a green door and a green roof. It has two trees in the garden and a red garden gate.

Student can be asked to write the other five paragraphs. They can even be asked to complete the sentences in a couple of paragraphs, like these:

(a) Sagar's house has .... windows and one_________ It has a_________ door and a_________roof. It has_________trees in the garden and a_________garden gate.

(b) _________house has one room and one window. It has a_________door and a red_________It has one_________in the garden and a_________garden gate.

The student can also be asked to colour the pictures of the six houses suitably, writing the name of the child in a box in each picture.

(1) Skimming

Read the paragraphs and write one word in each box.

- There are _______________ children.
- Each paragraph is about a _______________.
- Find two numbers. What are they?_______________ _______________
- Find two colours. What are they? _______________ _______________

(By completing this task, the students show that they have a good idea of the content of the six paragraphs or the tabular information).

(2) Scanning

Write child's name in each box. Do it as quickly as possible.

- His house has one window and a red roof. _______________
- Her house has one tree and a garden roof. _______________

Write a colour in each box. Do it as quickly as possible.

- Harsha's house has a _______________ garden gate.
- Shivam's house has a _______________ door.

(3) Matching

Match the picture given below with the children.

(The pictures of the six houses are drawn, but not in the order of the names given in the Table)

Write the child's name under each picture and colour the pictures.

(4) Making Inferences

Write a child's name in each box.

- His favourite colour is green. _______________
- His favourite colour is red. _______________

- Her house is very warm. ______________
- His house is very airy. ______________

(The teacher should ask the students to justify their responses, using language similar to that of the text as well as their own previous knowledge and experiences about warmth or airiness.)

Teacher may think of other ways of exploiting this material for reading. For example, teacher may ask comprehension question based on the tabular information, like, 'How many children have house with two rooms?' But teachers must not forget that every reading task set their students should have the clear aim of developing one or more of the specific sub-skills or reading like skimming, scanning or inferencing.

To get success in your studies, read only GPH book.

3 Activities—Speaking and Writing

An Overview

The main purpose of teaching and learning a language is to have a fluent communication with another person of the same language. In any language, the effective communication is done with the help of two different mediums. Just-like, while teachers teach English in India, take Hindi as another language. Both mediums of communication cannot be accomplished without the help of appropriate language. Therefore, the requirement of a language is must. These mediums also require some specific skills, without which communication cannot be done properly. Both the mediums share some of these skills.

Thus, in this chapter, we will study about the two basic skills, i.e. speaking and writing, without which the communication cannot be done properly. Both oral and written language is used for the purpose of communication. Thus, further, the characteristics and nature of spoken and written language, some approaches to teaching , classroom activities, emerging trends in teaching writing and teaching of English grammar will be studied in this chapter.

Q1. What are the similarities between spoken and written language?

Ans. The main purpose of language is to convey meaningful message. It doesn't matter whether language is in written or spoken form. These meaningful messages constitute an essential part of the communication process between speakers of a particular language. Thus, spoken as well as written languages have in common the communicative function. The language we use for communicating with others either through writing or speech is to a large extent determined by the context in which the interaction is taking place. It means that the relationship between participants, the location or setting in which the communication is taking place is the subject/topic on which the communication is based and the purpose for which the participants communicate. The entire context, thus, determines the style used for communication. Both mediums of communication use styles ranging from the very formal to the very informal. These styles are manifested in the language we use. Let us look at the following examples in the spoken medium.

Example 1:

Ragini	:	Dr. Prakash let me introduce you to Dr. Sharma. Dr. Puri. I'd like you to meet......
Dr. Prakash	:	How d'you do Dr. Sharma? Pleased to meet you.
Dr. Sharma	:	Hello, how d'you do?
Ragini	:	Dr. Sharma is a physicist. He works at theNational Physical Laboratories.
Dr. Prakash	:	Oh, I'm a pharmacist at IDPL.
Dr. Sharma	:	IDPL has been in the news for quite some time, hasn't it?
Dr. Prakash	:	Yes, we had closed for nearly a month. The employees were on strike.
Dr. Sharma	:	Has the problem been resolved?
Dr. Prakash	:	Yes, we resumed work last week.

Example 2:

Kajal	:	Suresh met my friend Lata.
Suresh	:	Hi! Are you the one who had an exhibition of your paintings last month?
Lata	:	Yes.
Suresh	:	I must say your paintings are wonderful.
Lata	:	Thanks. I'm planning another exhibition next year.
Suresh	:	That'll be lovely.

As is clear from the conversations, their main purpose is to introduce people to each other. But the two introductions differ from each other in some respects. These are minor as well as major differences.

We must have noticed that in the first conversation the style used to introduce the two people to each other is formal. In the second conversation it is informal. The persons introduced in the 'formal' conversation are addressed as 'Dr.' Prakash and 'Dr.' Sharma and not just by their first names. The persons in the second conversation on the other hand, are addressed by their first names and not their titles. We must also have noticed that the person doing the introductions in the first conversations has a formal relationship with the persons she introduces to each other. She is either junior to them in age or status or both. It is quite possible that she knows them at work as fellow scientists and they are not her friends. The introducer in the second conversation, on the other hand, obviously knows the two people she introduces very well. They are either her friends and/or class fellows or her relatives. Hence, she addresses them by their first names. The difference between the formal and the informal style can also be seen in the manner of greeting of the persons introduced. 'How d'you do?' is formal, whereas 'Hi!' is informal. The two pieces of conversation given above are only a sample of some of the difference between formal and informal oral interaction. Similar difference of style can be perceived in written language as well. Consider the following two examples of letters – one official and the other personal.

Example 1:

Address of sender
Address of addressee
Dear Dr. (Surname),

Thank you for your letter No... dated ..... I shall be glad to meet you and Shri .... to discuss details regarding the preparation of need based software for the Language Laboratory. It would be a good idea if you could meet me some time during the second half of September. Kindly let me know the days on which you propose to visit the Institute as soon as your programme is finalised.

With regards,
Yours sincerely,

....
Signature of sender

Example 2:

Address of Sender
Dear (first name)
Many thanks for your card. No, your off prints have not gone astray; as soon as I have finished typing out a tonal analysis of Punjabi, I shall settle down to studying them. A visit from our son and daughter-in-law in October, and from our daughter and son-in-law in November. Made a five-minute speech in Lapcha on 20 December, a lecture on the Rais in Darjeeling, for which I was made an honourary Bijuwa (witch-doctor) – my third doctorate!

Notice that the second letter ends abruptly without even the name of the person who had written it. The writer of the letter is obviously a friend of the addressee. Hence, it is the informal style. The first letter is addressed to a person not personally known to the sender. The communication is in response to a letter received by them from another institution. In contrast to the second letter, complete sentences are used and the letter begins with the addresses, and ends with 'Yours sincerely' and the signature of the sender. Sentences in the second letter are clipped. They convey messages that the writer intends to convey, nevertheless. The writer, being a friend of the receiver of the letter takes the liberty of communicating with her informally – a liberty that the writer of the formal letter cannot take. Thus, the relationship between the writer and addressee and the subject matter determine the form and style of the letter.

We have so far seen the spoken and written language both use different styles depending on the 'context' in which the communication takes place. The contexts we have looked at are only a sample of the numerous contexts that may form the basis for written and spoken communication.

Q2. Examine the differences between spoken and written language.

Or

Write a short note on distinction between writing and spoken language. [Dec-2012, Q.No.-1(c)]

Ans. There are two main sources from where the differences between spoken and written language arises. These are:

(1) Situational

When we use written language to communicate, we presume that the person(s) to whom the message is addressed is/are absent. In other words, written communication is essentially intended to convey messages to an audience that is absent, so that there is no face-to-face or direct interaction. Since the person(s) addressed is/are absent, it becomes necessary to be as explicit as possible by completing sentences carefully and precisely. Even in an informal letter like the one in the last section, the writer has used sentences (though clipped) and not just the odd word as in conversation. Spoken language on the other hand, presumes the presence of both the speaker and hearer. This makes it possible for them to support the word or phrase they utter by gesture, and be assured by word or look that their hearer has understood the message. In other words, feedback from the hearer is almost immediate. Spoken language, therefore, does not necessarily have to contain complete and well-formed sentences. This applies particularly to conversation. Also as a result of the difference owing to situation, writing tends to be relatively more permanent than conversation.

The second source of difference arises from the very nature of the devices used by the two mediums for the transmission of language. The device we use in the written medium comprises marks on the page which combine to form words and meaningful sentences. These orthographic signs are not adequate to represent the various devices we use to transmit language by speech. In other words, marks on the page do not give us any indication of how they are to be pronounced. Numerals in different language, for example, may be written in the same script and have the same value but are generally pronounced differently in different languages. For example, in French, German and English the numbers on the page are the same, that is, they are written thus – 1, 2, 3, 4, 5, 6, 7, 8, 9, 10, etc. but these numbers do not give us any clue as to how they are pronounced in these languages.

Similarly, many languages may use the same letters of the alphabet that is, the same script, e.g. English, German, French, Khasi and other tribal languages in the North East. However, these letters may not represent the same sounds in each of these languages, nor do they indicate the way in which the sounds in each language combine to form words and words combine to form longer utterances. In some languages, such as English, there is in fact not one-to-one correspondence between spelling and sound. In addition to the sound of each language, the rhythm of each language is different. Rhythm and intonation are properties spoken language alone and cannot be represented by sentences on the page.

(2) Societal

The societal functions of speaking and writing languages are quite separate. For examples, we can use only the spoken form of a language at interviews, for discussion on radio and television and in the classroom, at conferences, at seminars, for day-to-day interaction at the work place and at home and also for communication on the telephone. We can use only written language for report writing, for letter writing, for sending FAX, TELEX, E-Mail messages, etc. As a result of the separate functions (apart from the communicative function) that the two minds have various meanings in conversational English. In written English, on the other hand, each of the uses of these two words has a separate word. The word 'get' can mean 'receive' as in *Did you get my letter?* and understand in *Did you get what I said?* In written English, *get* can be substituted by *receive* in the first case and by *understand* in the second case.

Similarly, the two mediums tend to differ in respect of their structure. Let us look at some 'written' sentences with a 'translation' by M.A.K. Halliday (1985) into a form that would be more likely to occur in speech which is not specially 'colloquial'.

Table 3.1

Written	Spoken
(a) Investment in a rail facility implies a long-term commitment.	If you invest in a rail facility, this implies that you are going to be committed for a long term.
(b) The growth of attachment between infant and mother signals the first step in the development of a child's capacity to discriminate amongst people.	When an infant and its mother start to grow attached to each other, this is a sign that the child id beginning to discriminate amongst people.
(c) Slavish imitation of models is nowhere implied.	It is not implied anywhere that there are models which should be slavishly imitated.

In sentence (a), there are altogether ten words. Of these, seven, that is, *investment, rail, facility, implies, long, term* and *commitment* are lexical items and three, that is, *in, a* and *a* are grammatical items or structure words.

In the likely spoken form of the same sentence, words—*invest, rail, facility, implies, committed, long-term* are lexical items and the remaining thirteen are structure words. Similarly, in sentence (b), the 'written' sentence has twelve content words, out of which eleven are structure words. The likely spoken form of the sentences has ten content words and sixteen structure words.

The 'written' sentence (c) has four content words and three structure words. The likely spoken form of the same sentence has four content words and ten structure words.

In all these cases, the spoken form makes use of more structure words and fewer content words. The written sentence, on the other hand, makes use of a large number of content words. These contribute to the density with which information is presented in writing.

The presence of a larger number of grammatical words in spoken language makes it sparse. In other words, information in written language tends to be more closely packed than in spoken language.

Q3. Mention the essential features of spoken interaction. Giving the examples of a speaking activity mention what features of communication you would ask the students to bear in mind.

Or

"Spoken language differs from written language in many ways". Describe the characteristics/features of spoken language in the light of the above statement.

Or

Write a short note on characteristics of spoken language.

[June-2013, Q.No.-1(c)]

Ans. An important characteristic of spoken language is different in the styles of speech. These differences are dependent upon the total context in which interaction between people takes place. A context would be formal or informal in terms of the relationship between participants in an interaction, the locale or setting in which the interaction takes place and the purpose and topic of the interaction. A speaker's style would be formal, for example, at official meetings, conferences, seminars, etc. We might ask what is the difference between formal and informal styles of speech and how these are realised. Very often on a formal occasion, a speaker is well-prepared to speak, e.g. at seminars, conference, lectures and writes down what s/he has to say in detail. The speaker has already through about the subjects of the talk/paper, etc. and expresses himself/herself in language, which is similar to that of written prose. This has been called spoken prose.

Firstly, the vocabulary used would be related to the subject being spoken about, and therefore, be to some extent technical. Secondly, the structure of the sentences would be complex and packed with all the information the speaker wishes to convey. Owing to this explicitness, the speaker would probably have little or no hesitation, few gestures, few long pauses and complete sentences.

We all know that when learners start learning to use spoken language, they speak it in its most frequently used form, i.e. conversation. Conversation whether formal or informal requires:

- The ability to think on one's feet:
- Skill in the use of appropriate language:
- Skill in the use of devices that contribute to success in oral communication and help to make the speaker more fluent:

The ability to think on one's feet develops with experience and is enhanced by the development of skills mentioned in (ii) and (iii).

Thinking as we talk puts a limit on the time for deciding what to say and how to say it. To give ourselves a little time to decide, we generally use certain devices that facilitate this. Features here include the use of fillers, pauses hesitation. One kind of filler is the use of phrases like well, erm, you see, kind of, sort of, I mean, you know and so on. Another kind of filler arises when we repeat what we or others in the interaction have said. Also, we do not always use complete utterances. We abbreviate them by omitting unnecessary elements where possible. This is known as ellipsis. For example, a question like, *'Where've you come from?'* would get the response, *'Calcutta/Bombay/Dehradun', etc.* Or a question like *'Where did the monkey go?'* would probably get a response like *'up that tree or into that room'*. Another devices that helps a speaker in producing their message is the use of fixed conventional 'colloquial' or idiomatic expressions or phrases. These are sometimes called formulaic.

- I don't believe a word of it.
- Who does he think he is?
- Very nice to meet you.
- What can I do for you?

These expressions are more or less fixed and are learnt as whole and facilitate oral fluency.

As the spoken language takes place in the present, is generally not recorded and is only temporary. As a result, what is being communicated can be altered entirely or rephrased. In writing, such alterations are kept to minimum because too many of them may confuse readers. In speaking, however, rephrasing and alteration may even become necessary, so that listeners may have enough time to understand, and be reminded of things that were said in the course of interaction.

Thus, the processing conditions of spoken language result in certain common language features such as hesitations, self-corrections, rephrasings, ellipsis, repetition by expanding or reducing utterances, formulaic expressions.

Let's look at the following sample of spoken language which is a recording of a native speaker describing an accident.

S: 'It's erm - an interaction of kind of two - a kind of crossroads - of a minor road going across a major road - and I was standing there - and there was this erm - kind of ordinary car - on the minor road - just looking to come out - onto the big road - and coming down towards him on the big road was a van - followed by a lorry - now - just as he started to come out onto the main road - the van - no the lorry star - started to overtake the van - not having seen the fact that another car was coming out. '(from Brown and Yule 1983:140).

The "-" indicates that the speaker paused either to give himself enough time to think, or to rephrase what he has already said, or to correct himself or repeat himself to explain what he means.

The first question that we are likely to ask when we study the features of spoken language is, 'Why might these features be important for learners and why should we as teachers be aware of them?

- Firstly, these features act as facilitators for oral production. In other words, they help learners to process language so as to use it effectively for communication. It is important for learners to use these features to develop their speaking skill, because they may help learners to sound normal in their use of the foreign/ second language. They may also build up their confidence, and help them in becoming more fluent. If these features occur naturally in learners' speech, this may affect us as teachers, because it may have implications for the way learners should work. It would also influence what we as teachers expect of our learners in oral activities. We would not, for example, expect our learners to produce full sentences every time they open their mouths in the classroom. Moreover, in an interaction, we would not expect learners to repeat what is given the context all the time, for this would make is laborious, boring and unnatural. In addition, the occurrence of these features in learners' speech would also affect how we evaluate learners.
- In addition to the devices used by learners to enable them to think on their feet while interacting with others. Learners also need to use appropriate language. By appropriate, we mean language that will be meaningful in a given context. In other words, speaker and listener have to produce coherent language and be good at saying what they want to say in a way which the listener can understand the speaker. The development of skills in the use of devices for successful communication hinges on our understanding of what constitutes spoken interaction. We shall therefore, try and identify the purposes for which we generally use spoken interaction.

Q4. What is it that we use for oral interaction and the skills we require for communicating successfully?

Or

What are 'routines'? Which is/are the routine(s) that the students most require?

Ans. Firstly, it has been seen that in many circumstances, for conveying typical kinds of messages, speakers organise their utterances in typical patterns. These patterns correspond more or less to these kinds of message, and so deal with recurring cognitive problems. These have been called 'routines'. Examples of 'routines' include story telling or joke telling, descriptions, comparisons and instructions. Routines can be defined as 'conventional ways of presenting information'. Because they are conventional; they are predictable and help to ensure clarity. There are two main kinds of routines: information routines and interaction routines. By information routines, we mean frequently recurring types of information structures such as stories, descriptions of place and people, presentation of facts, comparisons, instructions. The principal types of information routines according to Brown and Yule (1983) are narration, description and instruction. Brown and Yule discuss narrative as an example of information routines and mention a certain number of essential components that narrative has, i.e. setting, time, participants, event, a point of view. In order to manage a story of any kind, the speaker must be able to give an economical but accurate account of each of these components. Such a task can get increasingly difficult with an increase in the number of elements under each of the categories mentioned above. For example, a story with more than one participant, with a setting that changes, with a changing time reference and with more than one event would be much more difficult to narrate.

Similarly, the description of an event, an accident, for example, can be made more difficult by increasing the number of cars, the number of directions in which vehicles go and the number of people involved. This aspect of complexity is one way in which teachers can develop and improve the skill of student in handling chunks of information.

The second kind of routines are based not so much on information content as on sequences of kinds of turns occurring in typical kinds of interaction likely to take place in given situations. Thus, 'service encounters' telephone conversations, interview situations, causal encounters, conversations at parties, radio or television interviews, conversations in class, all tend to be organised in characteristic ways. These routines can be seen as logical. However, the logical followed is based on what it makes sense to say before conversations, and farewells at the end. Telephone conversations reasonably begin by a check on who the other speaker is. Each of these conversations has a certain logical, although conversations may vary from one culture to another.

At this point, we might ask ourselves whether our students interact using both these kinds of routines and whether we need to develop the skills they require for communicating for these purpose. Very often in class, learners present facts, narrate incidents or stories, describe picture or processes, give instructions to juniors, discuss various issues that concern them. A large number of learners also need to interact with others on telephone, appear on television to interview someone or be interviewed, or even present programmes to a television audience.

Q5. How would you conduct a speaking activity to develop the skills of 'negotiating meaning'? Discuss both the pre-communicative and communicative stages.

Or

Write a short note on Negotiating meaning in a conversation.

[Dec-2012, Q.No.-1(d)]

Ans. In order to speak English well, that is, to communicate successfully in English, a learner has to produce grammatical utterances appropriate to the context in which they find themselves. In other words, the utterances must conform to the speaker's aim, to the role relationship between the interlocutors, to the setting, and the topic of conversation. Moreover, the learner must be able to produce their utterances within the time constraint imposed on them. Though they do not know in advance, what will be said to them, they must be able to respond fairly quickly, if they wish to continue the conversation.

Negotiating Meaning

Learners have to choose expressions that are appropriate to what the interlocutor knows and what s/he needs to know or can understand. For example, it is not good to speaking about our house to someone who does not know it in the same way as we would to someone who knows it well. Consider the situation that we have invited some friends to our place for a party. At one point, we require some teaspoons for dessert. Our guests happen to be in the kitchen chatting with us. We are unable to get to the drawer where they are kept. In the following examples, in one case we're speaking to our spouse, in another to a close friend, in another to a friend who has never been to our house and in one to a close friend, in another to a afraid friend who has never been to your house and in one to a foreign visitor. The following requests by us will be addressed to our different friend in different situations.

(1) You : Could you get me some teaspoons out of the drawer in the table please?

(2) You : Teaspoons, please.

(3) You : Do you think you could get me a dozen teaspoons? You'll find them in a drawer which is situated at the other end of the table.

(4) You : I need teaspoons for dessert. Could you get them for me? If you open the drawer you should find a cardboard box with the teaspoons. Would you mind?

As we must have noticed in each case that we give just as much information as is necessary for our various friends to respond. We would not get a response, for instance, if we said "Teaspoons, please" to our foreign visitor because that would not give him enough information to respond and to locate the teaspoons! In other words, the utterance would be obstructive to the natural flow of conversation, because the message is not explicit enough.

To negotiate meaning, we need to concentrate on how specific we are, in addition to the amount of information we communicate. Sometimes we find it sufficient to use a general term and to expand or modify and make it more precise later if the situation demands it. At other times, we may begin by being very precise and careful in our choice of words. When we want to give a definition of something for example, we may find the exact words, 'a frog is an amphibian'. At other times, we may use more than one word. To be responsible is for instance to 'let the other person know if we cannot for some reason keep an appointment we made.' Thus, learners would find various strategies to put across meaning useful. They would also find it useful to be aware of the importance of knowing various ways of getting things repeated or clarified or of clarifying and repeating things themselves. These help to maintain contact with the interlocutor(s) in an interaction and ensure understanding. For example, if a stranger asks us for directions, we would need to find out whether s/he knows anything at all about the city. If s/he is a tourist to the city, we would probably need to give him/her much more detailed information than we would give to someone who knows the city but not the particular place s/he has to go to. At every stage, in giving the stranger directions would involve checking that the other person has understood. The stranger who listens to the instructions would constantly be indicating by gestures and facial expression whether s/he has understood or not. S/he may check their understanding by repeating/summarising what we have said to them. S/he may ask questions for clarification and so on.

Precommunicative and Communicative Activities

A number of attempts have been made to classify exercises and activity types according to the aspects of conversational management and product they focus on. Littlewood (1981), for example, distinguishes four main kinds of activities:

Precommunicative activities	Communicative activities
Structural activities	Functional communicative activities
Quasi-communicative activities	Social-interactional activities

Precommunicative activities are those that deal with controlled practice of structures, conversation and include drills, dialogues and other exercises. Functional communicative activities concentrate on information transmission activities, whereas social-interactional activities are those that focus on social and cultural exchanges.

Q6. Describe the approaches to the teaching of conversation.

Or

Write a short note on Direct approach to teaching the speaking skill.
[Dec-2011, Q.No.-1(b)] [June-2012, Q.No.-1(d)]

Ans. The two approaches, i.e. direct and indirect focus on a different basis for the teaching of conversation. It would be responsible to select from each approach those aspects that would be suitable for the students.

Direct Approach

This approach to teaching conversation is one that focuses explicitly on the process and strategies involved in casual conversation. The programme, hence, concentrates on such aspects of conversation as strategies for turn-taking, topic control, conversational routines, fluency, pronunciation and differences between formal and causal conversational styles. To plan such a programme, one would be with the preparation of goals. Jack C. Richards (1990) provides the following samples, for example:

- How to use conversation for both transactional and interactional purposes?
- How to produce both short and long turns in conversation?
- Strategies for turn-taking in conversation.
- Strategies for opening and closing conversations.
- How to initiate and respond to talk on a broad range of topics and how to develop and maintain talk on these topics?
- How to use both a causal style of speaking and a neutral or more formal style?
- How to use conversation in different social settings and for kinds of social encounters, such as on the telephone, at informal and formal social gatherings?
- How to maintain fluency in conversation, through avoiding excessive pausing, breakdowns and errors of grammar or pronunciation?
- How to use conversational fillers and small talk?
- How to use conversational routines?

In planning and developing a programme, each goal can be described in more detail as a set of objectives. Each objective can in turn be specified in some detail by describing the kind of interaction to be taught and the performance level that is expected.

For example:

Level	:	basic
Objective	:	respond to requests for factual information
Content area	:	personal and family identification
Specific objectives	:	the learner will provide personal information in a simulated interview with a Government official.
Standards	:	responses to be comprehensible to someone used to dealing with a second language learner.

The example of specified objectives given above is only one of the approaches to goal and syllabus specification. Whatever approach we may adopt, recognition of these kinds of goals provides a basic for the design and selection of classroom activities and materials.

Indirect Approach

According to the research based on second language acquisition, the learners acquire language through conversation. In other words, one learns to interact verbally and syntactic structures are developed through this interaction. There is, thus, a close relationship between conversation and second language learning. The conversation class is one of the prime opportunities for learners to engage in natural conversation through the use of communicative tasks and activities. It is not necessary to teach conversation in any real sense. In practical terms, this leads to the use of pair-work and group-work activities that require learner-to-learner interaction. Tasks most likely to bring this about involve information sharing and negotiation of meaning. The focus is on using language to complete a task, rather than on practicing language for its own sake. However, there are obvious limitations to an exclusively task-based approach to teaching conversation. The first limitation according to reports of research on foreign language learning is that the interaction through communicative tasks may lead to language learning but does not guarantee grammaticality or sociolinguistic appropriateness. The studies seem to suggest that although communicative tasks may be a necessary component of a conversation programme, they are not a sufficient component.

Another limitation of a task-based approach to teaching conversation is that generally the communicative activities employed in task-based teaching, typically deal only with the transaction or information giving uses of language, but ignore the use of conversation to create social interaction and social relations. It is argued that these should find a central place in a conversational interaction. In order to ensure that this happens, a direct attempt to teach strategies for conversational interaction is also needed. To get success in your studies, read only GPH Book.

Q7. In your own teaching, what do you emphasise: fluency or accuracy. Why?

Or

What according to you, should be emphasised when you are teaching student how to speak with fluency or accuracy? Give reasons for your answer. [Dec-2010, Q.No.-4][June-2011, Q.No.-4]

Ans. The overall goal behind giving the activities and tasks to teach conversation is, to help the learner produce fluent speech. Some describe fluency as "reasonable speech; with sufficient precision, with reasonable correctness (grammatically, lexically, phonologically)." Fluency is also described as "the ability to fill time with talk... the ability to talk in coherent reasoned and semantically dense sentences showing a mastery of the semantic and syntactic of the language", "the ability to have appropriate things to say in a wide range of contexts." According to others, "fluent speech is the cumulative result of dozens of different kinds of processes". Although fluency is difficult to define clearly; it is important in the context of learning/teaching the spoken language.

The concept of fluency is a reflection of the main objective of the speaker to produce speech that is easy to follow, free from errors and breakdowns in communication and acceptable in both content and form, though this goal is often not met due to processing condition of spoken language result in certain common language features such as the processing and production demands on the speaker. The processing conditions of spoken language result in certain common language features such as hesitations, ellipsis, repetition, etc. and that the production of speech in real time imposes pressures. Accuracy generally includes control of grammar and pronunciation. It is seen as a component of fluency rather than as an independent dimension of conversational skill. The kind of discourse speakers produce and the degree of fluency they achieve generally depend upon the task they are attempting and the context for communication, that is whether they are participating in an interview or in a discussion, or whether they are involved in narrating a story, or giving a description, for answering questions or even giving a definition. In an interview or in a discussion, for example, a speaker would be required to think on his feet and produce spontaneous utterances and would, therefore, make greater use of devices that facilitate production, than a speaker narrating a story. In narrating a story, a speaker would have thought about the story and his/her utterances would be more planned and have fewer hesitations, and thus, be more fluent.

Q8. "While developing the spoken skills of learner, a teacher must create a need for communication." Explain with the help of an activity or a communication game.

Ans. Of course, no matter what efforts we make, classroom setting can never provide students with authentic context as in real communication environment. But still we must try to let the students feel they are really doing some task, performing speech acts in the way it should be. When people ask question, it is often because they don't know the answer or it may be due to some other reason. When they speak or write, it is because they have something to say; and when they listen or read, they do it to get information or ideas. In other words, there is a need and a purpose for communication and something to be communicated. This need, purpose and substance are what gives rise to communication in real life. And, therefore, these communicative situations are what we try to provide our students with when we want them to speak, write, listen or read. However, we should take care not to make students ask such obvious questions as 'Is this a book' when everybody can see it is a book, or to ask each other 'what is your name?' When they already know each other's names. This kind of speaking is not 'spoken' English. Spoken English means communicating something through the spoken mode.

An instance of this is classroom discourse, i.e. getting things done in the class—mainly as a means of communication. Something real communicative situation develop spontaneously, as in exchanging comments on last night's TV programme or someone's new dress, hair style, etc. The majority of language teaching situations before reaching an advanced level, however, are geared towards structure-oriented communication. Since foreign language, situations in which real communication occurs naturally have to be suitably created in the classroom.

Activity

Look at the three short conversations given below and discuss or say:

- in what situation each conversation might take place in real life;
- why the person might be asking the question.

Consider the following questions and their expected answers:

(i) What's Ruby doing?
She is doing her homework.

(ii) Can you type letter?
Yes I can.

(iii) What is there in the room?
There is a table and two chairs and a single bed.

There are of course many possible answers of the above questions.

- Father asking mother about daughter – he has just arrived home and she is not in the room, so he wonders where she is.
  - A friend calling at Ruby's house and asking her mother – she wants to go out with her.
- Someone being interviewed for a job (e.g. as a secretary) the interviewer needs to know because the job involves typing.
  - Someone enquiring about a room which they want to rent, or someone booking a room in a hotel; they want to know if it is suitable.

From the above activity, a few main points can be established:

In all the conversations, the two people are genuinely information. There is something that one person does not know and wants to find out, and that is why s/he is asking a question. We can say that the person has a communicative need.

Although this is not the only reason why people communicated in real life, it is one of the main reasons; very often we talk in order to tell people things do not know, or to find out things from other people.

Q9. How appropriacy, authenticity and globalness are interrelated?

Ans. In a real life situation, when we ask questions, people have the freedom to answer as they choose, so there is always an element of unpredictability.

In the traditional textbooks, however, when the students are called upon to answer questions, they are often instructed to give only affirmative or negative answers or full or short answers. That cannot be counted as communication, since communication involves freedom and unpredictability. As teachers of English, it becomes necessary for us to create situations in a classroom where we give students an opportunity to respond to a particular situation with the help of language inputs which s/he has already mastered. An amount of 'controlled' freedom in a situation will have to be provided, so that the students learn to "communicate".

There is another important point which a language teacher has to bear in mind, and that is making students learn through use, naturally implies that the target language they come into contact with should be real, that is authentic, appropriate and global.

By authentic language, one does not mean, the language spoken by native speakers. In fact, it means language that is actually used in real communicative situations, as opposed to language that is artificially made up for purpose other than communication.

For example consider the following dialogue:

Teacher	:	Good morning, everybody
Students	:	Good morning, Mam.
Teacher	:	Well, how are you all, today?
Students	:	Fine, thank you mam. And what about you Geeta? How are You?
Geeta	:	I'm well, thank you, Mam.
Teacher	:	Good.

The teacher asked Geeta individually, after she had asked the whole class how they were. Perhaps the teacher wants to bring in an authentic situation in the classroom, when students will speak English, therefore, she did this.

And, therefore, authentic language naturally entails appropriacy. Appropriacy is part of authenticity, not only of the language used, but also of the situation and role, is another practice that appropriacy can be learnt and taught. On the other hand, if language is taught through and for use, appropriacy is something which we cannot be ignored.

'Globalness' of language means that it is whole and multi-dimensional, in which all sorts of forms may occur naturally as the occasion requires. Hence, as teachers of English, we will have to bear in mind these points-namely that we have to create a need for communication. Students have to be taught language which they can use with freedom in an unpredictable situation. And these unpredictable situations have to be authentic situations, where all forms of language occur in its natural forms.

Q10. What are the ways of bringing communicative situations in the classroom? Suggest some useful games.

Or

Write a short note on use of Ice-breakers in the class.

Or

Write a short note on communication games in the classroom.

Or

Write a short note on warm-up activities and ice-breakers.

[June-2012, Q.No.-1(f)]

Ans. As a teacher of English, one may like to try out or adapt following simple yet useful games in his/her classrooms. A teacher always needs to keep in mind the function of warm-up activities. These activities motivate the students towards learning the language. These exercises can provide an excellent means of breaking the ice, of shaking away the immediate previous experiences the group has been subjected to, of generating some fun and energy and claiming involvement from the whole class. These activities are simple, demand no factual learning and give a good opportunity for developing a "speaking situation" and spontaneity. If these activities are taken up in the beginning of the lesson, they are spontaneity. If these activities are taken up in the beginning of the lesson, they are called "Warm-up activities".

Given below are some of the more regularly used activities, which have survived most of the classrooms. Their common feature is that they can all be undertaken very easily with chairs and desks with very little movement of the students.

(1) Newspaper Headlines: Suppose we have to take up a mystery story in the classroom. How will we introduce it to the students? One way may be that we write the following headlines on the blackboard or collect newspaper headlines and show them to the students.

UFO's sighted	**Baby's doll found**
Man disappeared from the street	**Aliens visited the Earth**

Ask students to discuss the above headlines in pairs. Then two or three pairs can report to the class what they have discussed. Then ask them to read the story silently. This could be termed as a warm-up exercise.

(2) Talking Him Down: In this activity, everybody has a partner who is both close to and faces him/her. Holding eye contact the whole time, both are asked to talk to each other at the seconds, then a minute. The aim is to keep on talking at all costs and to make the other person dry up. No physical contact should be made, only talk used. A partner should not only hear a word that the person is saying but must concentrate on his/her own story also. A good starting point may be "Everything that happened to me from the time I woke up this morning". Other suggestions may be "Tell your favourite fairy story, with as much expression and animation as possible" or "Try to sell some kind of product".

It is a short activity. The first phase may be of thirty seconds and second may be of a minute. This activity generates a lot of noise, and laughter, students can overcome their initial inhibition in the racket and soon get tired of shouting. This activity could also to be used as an ice-breaker.

(iii) Colour Clash: Players work in pairs, each partner choosing a different colour which s/he says is his/her favourite. After a minute of 'thinking', each student turns to his/her own colour is far better and is one that should be adopted. Any argument or means of persuasion can be used.

This sounds straightforward enough but many students find that as they try to persuade the other person, they become more convinced of the validity of their own colour; then more complex arguments are generated. Colour is a rather personal matter and there can often be rich material which is created. We may use flattery, bribery and more subtle means of persuasion rather than confrontation, and this technique of communication can be further explore and illustrated.

(vi) Gentle Persuasion: Get the students to work in pairs and decide who is **A** and **B**.

(a) **A** sits on a chair and **B** has to stand up. Within two minutes, **B** has to use any means whatsoever, expect physical violence to persuade **A** to give up his/her chair so that **B** can sit on it. Pool back results and the way it was tackled.

(b) Now **A** to do the persuading. S/he has to imagine that s/he has some unusual attribute or qualities and has to persuade **B,** who will be full of doubt and questions.

Some more examples could be taken up:

(a) Persuade your partner to turn the TV over to a programme that you want to watch.

(b) Persuade your brother/sister to lend you the thing s/he treasures most.

(c) Persuade your father to increase your pocket money to cope with inflation.

(d) Persuade the bus conductor to let you travel home even though you have no money.

These exercises call for more ingenuity and invention. They aim within the pressure of limited time to cause the persuader to push his/her ideas thoroughly. All the different means of persuasion need to be explored here in pooling back, and new ones suggested.

(5) Communications: A series of short exercises to be tried in pairs to explore various means of communication in the class.

(a) **A** and **B** sit back to back, heads are not to be twisted around but must remain looking in opposite directions. They talk together about what they did over the weekend.

(b) **A** and **B** sit face-to-face but cannot speak or hear. **B** has a problem and tries to convey it to by mime while **A** attempts to help.

(6) Word Associations: First person starts with a noun (say 'table'), second person quickly says the first association s/he makes with that (say 'books') a third adds (say 'stories') and so on.

(7) Commentaries:

(a) These can all be single person activities. Players pretend they have a microphone or a telephone and give a running commentary into it like a radio sports commentator.

(b) Driving a car, giving commentaries of what the driver is doing, with all the sounds of the car's operation.

Q11. Write a short note on Simulation and Role-play. What are the basic patterns underlying role-play?

Ans. Role-playing, as an educational approach, is often referred to in the same context as simulation. However, the use of role-plays in teaching has received far less attention. Collectively, simulations and role-playing provide students with some form of imaginary or real world within which to act out a given situation. Beyond this, however, each is quite distinct. The aim of a simulation is to deepen students' conceptual understanding by working within, and reflecting upon, a representation of the real environment.

These methods of teaching are tremendously helpful methods for L2 learning. These help in encouraging thinking and creativity, let students develop and practice new language and behavioural skills in a relatively non-threatening setting, and can create the motivation and involvement necessary for learning to occur.

Teachers of English have turned to simulation activities and within this more to role-playing, in looking for ways of creating more varied forms of interaction in the classroom. The rationale behind role-play and simulation is the oral practice of the language. Situations are created in the classroom, so that students can act out their roles. In role-playing, the cue cards or role cards are given to the students as language inputs, whereas in simulation activities, the students have to imagine their part and then act in the class. The situations selected are from real-life in which a student is placed everyday.

Thus, there is a difference between simulations (where students act out real-life situations, for example the student checks in at "the airport", but students do play themselves) and role-plays where students take on different characters. In a role-play, for example, one student may be asked to take on the role of "an angry landowner", which is concerned with discussing the possible construction of a new road. Another may be asked to play the role of the "road company representative". Role-plays will thus require more "imagination" on the part of the student to be able to get "into" the role.

The basic patterns underlying role-play are as follows:

- Learners' focus is more firmly on the communication of meanings, rather than on the practice of language.
- Learners' identity with their roles in the interaction is deeper than during controlled language practices. If they do not, they will not be able to identify with the meanings being communicated through these roles. They learn to create new interactions themselves, on the basis of their roles and the meanings that arise, rather than perform in ways that have been predetermined by the teacher.

Q12. Write a short note on the role of teacher in communicative classroom.
[June-2011, Q.No.-1(c)][June-2012, Q.No.-1(b)]

Ans. Teachers have the responsibility to be a great leader in the classroom and to many groups of people. Presence of a teacher in the classroom should create a congenial atmosphere for a healthy teaching-learning process. In communicative activities, the teacher's role is definitely more as a facilitator, guide, monitor and as a general organiser. It should not be an authoritarian know-it-all role. There are some of the suggestions given by Littlewood regarding the role of the teacher:

As a general overseer of his/her students learning process, the teacher must aim to coordinate the activities so that they form a coherent progression, leading towards greater communicative ability.

- As a classroom manager, s/he is responsible for grouping activities into lessons and for ensuring that these activities are satisfactorily organised at a practical level.
- In many activities, s/he may not intervene after initiating the processing but will let learning take place through independent activity or pair/group work.
- When such an activity is in progress, s/he may act as a consultant

or adviser, helping wherever necessary. S/he may also move around the classroom in order to monitor the strengths and weaknesses of the learners, as a basis for planning future learning activity.

- S/he will something wish to participate in an activity as co-communicator with the learners. In this role, s/he can simulate and present new language without taking the main initiative for learning away from the learners themselves.

Q13. Write a short note on the nature of writing.

Or

"The art of writing differs from the craft of writing." Explain using the example of a writing task. [Dec-2012, Q.No.-4]

Ans. "Writing is a creative process where one discovers oneself... it is a process of reaching out for one's thoughts and discovering them. Writing, as such, is a process of meaning making."

— ***Third Year Degree Student (Singapore)***

The process of learning to write is lifelong. Writing has its moments of **ecstasy** as well as agony. We develop a love-hate relationship towards writing, for it is a **painful** pleasure.

It is often wrongly assumed that a good speaker is a good writer. This need not necessarily be so, for, speech and writing are different modes of communication. Writing is much more than a mere transcription of speech. Speech is **natural** and **instinctive**; all normal human beings learn to speak their mother tongue; but not everyone masters writing, even in his/her mother tongue. The writer often lacks the aids to communication that are available to a speaker.

Harold Rosen remarks, "The writer is a lonely figure.... He writes with one hand tied behind his back, being robbed of gesture. He is robbed too of the tone of his voice.... He is condemned to monologue, there is no one to help out, to fill the silences, put words in his mouth, or make encouraging noises."

Of the four language skills, writing is the most complex and difficult. It requires an active command of vocabulary, grammatical patterns and sentence structures. It demands the mastery of conventions of writing like spelling and punctuation. Even more importantly, it calls into play a high degree of organisation, which is essential to achieve coherence in what one says. The salient features of writing may be represented as follows:

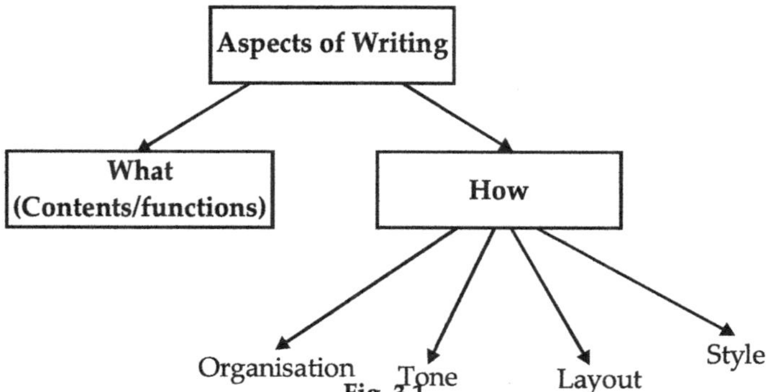

Fig. 3.1

While answering the question, "What skills do good writers demonstrate?" Tricia Hedge distinguishes between the 'art' of writing and the 'craft' of writing, which are elaborated as below:

The 'Art' of Writing: Authoring Skills

- having something to say (a sense of purpose)
- being aware of the reader (a sense of audience)
- working from first to final draft (a sense of process)
- developing the ideas (a sense of direction)

The 'Craft' of Writing: Crafting skills

- organising the content clearly and in a logical manner
- manipulating the script (handwriting)
- using the conventions (e.g.) spelling, lay out
- getting the grammar right
- developing sentence structure
- linking ideas
- using a range of vocabulary.

Ann Raimes (1983: 6) presents the various **aspects** of writing in the form of a diagram:

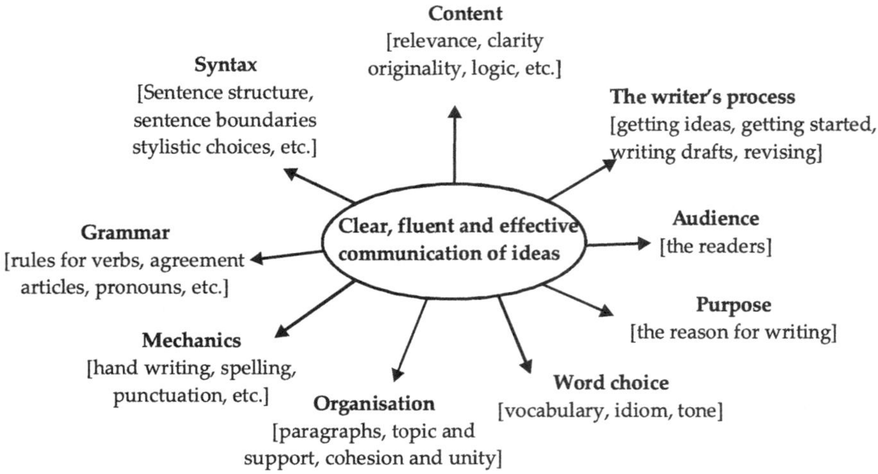

Fig. 3.2

The purpose of writing consists of three important phases, i.e. pre-writing, writing and re-writing and editing. In the pre-writing or planning stage, the writer identifies his subject and generates ideas, selects and organises them. In this process, she attempts to answer two questions: Why am I writing this? Who am I writing this for? This enables him/her to fix the context, and thus, achieve a sense of audience and purpose.

The second stage of writing and rewriting the first draft is quite complex. It is often interrupted. The writer stops, reads over what she has already written, revises, brings in new ideas or re-arranges them. While the first phase focuses on WHAT the writer wants to say, in this phase, the focus shifts towards HOW to say it effectively.

In the third stage of editing, the writer attempts to assess his/her writing from the reader's perspective; s/he makes final adjustments and checks accuracy in spelling, grammar, punctuation, etc.

Q14. What do you understand by the process-oriented approach to writing? Provide a plan of activities you would undertake to help learners attempt a writing task. [June-2013, Q.No.-4]

Or

What do you understand by the process approach to writing? How is it different from the other approaches? Give reasons. [June-2012, Q.No.-4]

Or

In what way is the process-approach to writing more meaningful than the model-based approach? Give examples to elucidate your point.

Ans. The Process-Oriented Approach

Writing is often regarded as a thinking process. A writer goes through various processes when s/he writes a piece of composition. These are thinking, organising ideas, considering the context and redrafting. However, it is not a linear process as it is often assumed to be. It is a hierarchical process in which different events needs not to take place in a sequential order. For instance, in the process of redrafting, s/he may stumble upon a new idea. Skilled writers do have a tentative plan, which keeps changing as they write. In order to arrive at the final product, (an essay, an article, etc.) good writers adopt various processes. They plan, generate ideas, craft, read, raise and rewrite. Our learners will also learn to write better if we guide them through these various processes. The process approach is a learner-centered approach. It models the writing process rather than the written product. It involves the active participation of learners and focuses on how to write rather than what to write.

The Model Based Approach

Here the pupils are provided with a model text. They analyse the elements of the text and then write a parallel passage. Models are very helpful to weak learners; they do not know how to write on their own, and the models provide them good support. However, bright pupils often feel unhappy with models since it gives them no scope for originality or creativity. Hence, models have to be used judiciously. Originally, the models are presented first and the approach may be represented as follows:

Study the Model - Analyse the Elements - Produce a Parallel Text

We can make the approach more challenging for the pupils by adopting the following procedure:

Specify task à Let learners write what they can à Study model à Compare with learner's writing à Revise

The presentation of the model, in the context of his/her own writing, especially after his/her initial struggle is sure to be much more meaningful and useful for the learner.

Plan of activities

- This provides support through ideas, visuals, hints, tables, diagrams, etc. We shall look at a set of graded tasks to train a learner to write a descriptive paragraph.
- Motivate learners by asking them to write on authentic real life contexts. Provide them with a reader and purpose.
- Don't give the rules. Let the learners discover the rules on their own. Adopt a problem-solving approach. Exploit what they know.
- Make writing interactive. Integrate the skills of listening, speaking, reading and writing.

Q15. Write a short note on interactive approach to teaching writing.
[Dec-2011, Q.No.-1(c)][Dec-2012, Q.No.-1(e)]

Ans. The major aim of language teaching is to develop in our learners the ability to communicate in English; and communication involves interaction.

Unless there is interaction, we cannot have proper communication. To promote interaction, we have to make sure that there is lively attention and active participation by learners. Interactive activities may take the form of pair work, group work, etc. We could even design tasks where a learner interacts with a text, and works on his/her own. In the traditional classrooms, we have only one type of interaction - where the teacher interacts with the whole class; this is highly teacher dominated, since learners are expected to speak only when the teacher asks them to do so.

Interactive tasks create a relaxed atmosphere in the classroom. Further, learners do not feel lonely or threatened. They begin to enjoy composition classes. They learn from each other and work without a sense of inhibition. In the process of interacting, they acquire fluency in communication. They also get practice in all the four skills - listening, speaking, reading and writing; or rather, they learn to write through listening, speaking and reading.

Q16. Briefly describe the major approaches to teaching grammar.

Or

Which is/are the best approach(es) to the teaching of grammar? Why? What are the steps you take to teach a grammar lesson effectively? [Dec-2010, Q.No.-5]

Ans. Teaching English grammar can be hard going for the teacher and the students. It doesn't have to be difficult or painful, however. We can teach English grammar using fun learning games and before we know it our students will be more than willing.

There are three major approaches to teaching grammar. These are discussed as follows:

(a) Formal Presentation of Grammatical rules

Traditional teachers of English followed this approach to grammar teaching. There are several grammar books, which present the rules of English grammar, e.g. Wren and Martin, Nesfield, etc. These rules are prescriptive; while they have their own value, we should be careful not to exaggerate their importance. For, some of these rules are no longer valid; if we continue to follow them, our English would sound quite funny. There is an interesting anecdote of how Churchill was once asked to observe the rule "A sentence should not end with a preposition". He retorted by saying, "This is a rule which I cannot put up with". The mastery of the rules of grammar will surely make our learners veterans in grammar; they will be able to answer the questions on grammar well and secure full marks in the grammar section of the paper. But when they speak or write, they generally forget the rules they learn and commit numerous mistakes. Hence, they are not able to communicate effectively in English outside the classroom.

(b) Practice of Common Grammatical Patterns

In this approach, students are not taught the rules or grammar; they are merely asked to practice the structures of language. They are given substitution tables which drill them in the correct use of structures. It is, thus, impossible for them to come out with an ungrammatical sentence. For example, consider the following table and make sentences using the table:

I They Smita Rakesh	like	mangoes

Such drilling helps students to become familiar with the basic patterns in English. However, it does not tell them when to use these patterns. There is also the danger that they may mechanically repeat the sentences without understanding the grammatical rules involved.

(c) Providing Opportunities to Use English in Realistic Situations

In this approach, the teacher is not concerned with teaching grammar in the form of rules of drill. His/her major objective is to create opportunities for the learners to communicate in English. It is believed that by engaging in the process of communication, the students will implicitly master the rules of grammar. Hence, the more opportunities learners get for communication, the better their proficiency. We should not, however, imagine that the teacher would allow the students to speak or write ungrammatically. When learners come out with ungrammatical sentences, the teacher will provide the correct form incidentally. S/he will not immediately start a remedial grammar lesson in that area. The basic belief of this approach is that learners learn by doing, i.e. they learn to communicate by communicating, and not by mastering a set of rules or repeating a set of patterns. Though these learners will develop fluency, it is possible that they will not know how to explain the grammatical rules of English.

Q17. Is teaching grammar necessary in the class? If so, why? Briefly discuss the stages of a grammar lesson using any grammar item of your choice.

Or

What are the components of a grammar lesson based on the plan of Calce Murcia and Hiller?

Ans. Grammar is innermost to the teaching and learning of languages. It is also one of the harder aspects of language to teach well. Many people, including language teachers, hear the word "grammar" and think of a fixed set of word forms and rules of usage. They associate "good" grammar with the prestige forms of the language, such as those used in writing and in formal oral presentations, and "bad" or "no" grammar with the language used in everyday conversation or used by speakers of non-prestige forms.

Language teachers who adopt this definition focus on grammar as a set of forms and rules. They teach grammar by explaining the forms and rules and then drilling students on them. This results in boredom, disaffected students who can produce correct forms on exercises and tests, but consistently make errors when they try to use the language in context. Other language teachers, influenced by recent theoretical work on the difference between language learning and language acquisition, tend not to teach grammar at all. Believing that children acquire their first language without overt grammar instruction, they expect students to learn their second language in the same way. They assume that students will absorb grammar rules as they hear, read and use the language in communication activities. This approach does not allow students to use one of the major tools they have as learners: their active understanding of what grammar is and how it works in the language they already know.

Traditionally, it felt that it was not possible for a learner to speak or write English correctly if s/he did not know the grammar in English. However, modern ELT experts feel that a knowledge of grammar may not be necessary for one to communicate in a language. As evidence, they cite the example of a child acquiring its first language. The child is able to speak the language grammatically by the age of five, second language learner can also acquire a language without learning grammar. Widdowson, a famous applied linguist, holds a similar view. He feels that second language learners do not benefit from a knowledge of grammar, because they are not able to transfer this knowledge to their own communication. In other words, they are not able to apply or used their grammatical knowledge to actual situations of communication. Network goes to the extent of suggesting that a knowledge of grammar is neither necessary nor sufficient for language learners. First language learners find grammar unnecessary; they are able to communicate even without knowing any grammar. Second language learners find a knowledge of grammar insufficient, for even after learning grammar for several years, they are not able to speak or write grammatically.

The grammar has an important place in the English curriculum and it has to be taught for the following reasons:

- The purpose of learning any language is to acquire the ability to speak/write it grammatically, that is, grammar construction. Hence, every learner should have at least an implicit of grammar.
- Most of the English syllabi in India give considerable importance of grammar, hence, we have to teach 'grammar' whether we like it or not.
- Learners demand grammar. When we tell them they are wrong, they want to know why. Hence, grammatical explanation has to come in.

- Second language learners cannot have as much exposure to English as first language learners. A knowledge of grammar may help them to compensate for this lacuna.

Stages of Grammar Lesson

According to Celce Murcia and Hiller a grammar lesson consists of four parts:

(1) **Presentation:** The teacher selects a grammar structure relevant to student needs and introduces it. The teacher could present the structure.

For example:

- The passive in a natural context.
- My book was stolen.

She could then elicit the rule for forming the passive.

(2) **Focused Practice:** In this stage, students get practice in the use of the passive, through various exercises the teacher gives them the correct answers and also discusses their errors.

(3) **Communicative Practice:** Now, the learner engages in communicative activities to practise the structure that has been learnt. These activities are similar to communication in real life. There is a genuine information gap as in real life the learners have the choice, i.e. the freedom to say what they also get feedback from their peers regarding the effectiveness of their communication.

(4) **Teacher Feedback and Correction:** Although it has been listed last, feedback and correction actually form an integral part of all the three stages above. The teacher should not merely point out the error and correct it; instead, s/he should provide a cognitive challenge to the learners and provide them opportunities to discover their own mistakes.

Q18. Briefly describe the current trends in teaching grammar.

Or

With practical examples, show how you would use the following approaches to teaching grammar:

(a) teaching grammar in context, and

(b) teaching grammar as discourse.

[June-2011, Q.No.-4][Dec-2011, Q.No.-2][June-2012, Q.No.-2]

Or

What does teaching 'grammar in context' mean? Taking any grammar item from your school syllabus provide a plan of a grammar lesson to exemplify the approach. [Dec-2012, Q.No.-5]

Or

Write a short note on Grammar for Communication.

[June-2013, Q.No.-1(e)]

Ans. The teaching of grammar has undergone a tremendous change in present time. We shall briefly outline the basic principles below:

(a) Teach Grammar in Context

Most of our time-tables allocate a separate period for grammar. We select a particular area of grammar and teach the various aspects. Most often students feel bored with this, because they do not understand its relevance to real life contexts. They are often puzzled and confused. After all, there is no difference between saying *"I ate a mango"* and *"A mango was eaten by me"*, when they both mean the same thing. A little more planning will make the class more interesting. For example, passives may be taught through the context of laboratory reports or newspaper reports where the agent is not important. The present continuous tense may be presented in the context of running commentaries for cricket, tennis, etc.

(b) Focus on Fluency First and Accuracy Later

We, English teachers, on the whole feel very possessive about English grammar. If anyone makes a grammar mistake (whoever it may be) we have to point it out immediately, otherwise our conscience troubles us! But we should think of the effect of such correction on our learners who are just beginning to struggle to communicate. The moment we point out a mistake, they feel humiliated and inhibited. They feel it is better not to speak, rather than speak ungrammatically. Hence, it is advisable to pretend to ignore their mistakes in the early stages of learning. After they gain some fluency and confidence, we could slowly begin to emphasise the need for accuracy.

(c) Teach Grammar for Communication — Not Grammar for its Own Sake

Our aim in teaching is to help learners to communicate effectively. We are not interested in producing grammarians. Students may be very good in grammar when they do isolated exercises on grammar; but they often fumble and commit mistakes when they attempt to speak or write independently. We want our learners to acquire knowledge of language and not knowledge about language. It is not necessary for them to know what a noun or a verb is; they can still communicated without such knowledge. Hence, let us not frighten our learners with excessive use of grammatical labels. An analogy might help us to understand this better. If we want to learn driving, it is not necessary for us to understand this each part of the car. That is a mechanic's duty. We can still drive a car without knowing, for example, what the different parts of the engine are. Similarly, we can still speak/write a language without an explicit knowledge about grammar.

(d) Teach Grammar as Discourse — Not Isolated Sentences

The traditional grammar books present numerous exercises, which consist of isolated sentences, unconnected with each other. This is artificial and unrealistic. In real life, we always speak/write in continuous stretches of language classes, which should help our learners to communicate effectively in real life, then we should also give them practice in the use of continuous discourse.

(e) Make Grammar Learning Fun

Interactive games for grammar are very popular now. They motivate learners highly and help them to shed inhibitions. Games also help learners to practice the relevant structures without even being conscious of the fact that they are learning grammar.

Q19. In what sense is reading called a psycholinguistic guessing game? Explain monitoring the knowledge and skills one requires to arrive at the meaning of a text. [June-2013, Q.No.-3]

Ans. Reading is a complex cognitive process of decoding symbols for the purpose of deriving meaning (reading comprehension) and/or constructing meaning. It is the mastery of basic cognitive processes to the point where they are automatic so that attention is freed for the analysis of meaning.

In order to understand how second language learners handle reading; one must first establish how they may be considered to process text at a cognitive level. After establishing that reading depends on parallel 'top-down' and 'bottom-up' processing, we go on to consider the main factors that contribute to reading fluency and vocabulary acquisition; and we also cover the related aspects of teaching and learning practice that may contribute to developing these aspects of L2 reading skills. We then consider the role-played by top-down factors: self-monitoring, awareness of text types and background knowledge.

'Top-down' models of reading were popular from the 1970s, the most frequently cited example of this approach being Goodman (1967): 'Reading: A Psycholinguistic Guessing Game'. In classroom practice, this widely replaced the 'bottom-up' models that had been in use, and in which the reader deals with letters, words and sentences in rank order, each step depending on the preceding one. Top-down models assume that the reader interrogates the text rather than processing it completely, getting meaning by comparing expectations to a sample of information from the text.

Exclusively top-down models have been definitively falsified by empirical studies showing that skilled readers do not sample portions of the text, but rather process the entire text, rapidly and automatically. In currently accepted evidence-based models of reading, bottom-up processes (like word recognition and lexical access) and top-down processes (like integrating background knowledge) proceed in parallel (Rumelhart 1977, Stanovich 1980). Both sorts of processes are vital to skilled reading. The degree to which lower- and higher-level capacities may come into play in this interactive process may well differ, according to the purpose for reading. Looking quickly over a text, either to decide whether to read it or for gist (skimming) or looking for specific information in a text (scanning), will not require the same mix as reading for general understanding or pleasure. Intensive reading (i.e. critical reading or reading to learn) will require yet a different balance between the two processes (Urquhart and Weir 1998:46). Higher-level processes may be best developed through intensive reading, for this focuses on aspects of the text and on the conscious use of strategies. The typical intensive reading text will be just above the level at which the reader can easily read.

However, for all types of reading, the reader needs automaticity both of word recognition and of lexical access (recognising the word so as to find its meaning in memory, and silently activating its pronunciation). When a word is recognised, it enters the phonological loop of working memory, becoming available for consultation and integration into a mental representation of the text (Gathercole and Baddeley 1995). The faster a reader's speed of retrieval from the mental lexicon, which is linked to their level of vocabulary knowledge, the more proficient their reading comprehension will be. These features are treated below in terms of fluency and vocabulary.

The Book you can believe most - GPH book.

4 Creating Materials

An Overview

The nature and qualities of the teaching materials that teachers use can have a substantial effect on the educational experience of their students. Teaching materials can often distract learners rather than help them to learn. Common avoidable problems include overcrowded or illegible slides, irrelevant or badly prepared handouts, and incompatible multimedia equipment. It is important, therefore, to know how to create effective teaching materials. Besides teachers, parents are also very conscious about the studies of their children. The very first thing parents do, when a child is admitted in a new class, is the purchasing of his/her course books. Thus, teachers should be effective in teaching the course books of their students, as the course books are the centre of general attention of both teachers as well as students. Thus, the course material for studies becomes an important aspect of our formal education system.

Q1. What do you understand by teaching materials? Discuss the usefulness of instructional materials.

Or

Discuss the role-played by the learning material in the classroom.

Or

Write a short note on Developing instructional materials.

[Dec-2011, Q.No.-1(e)]

Ans. Course books, teaching materials or learning materials has an important role in learning-teaching process. Textbooks help the teacher in planning his/her lesson in a systematic way. They span out course content in a manner that is useful to the examiner in preparing a comprehensive and reliable question paper. Though, all this is quite obvious, but we can also think of useful materials other than books. Printed materials (books or any other printed matter), the most commonly used materials, are considered as only one type; others are audio and video materials. Many courses include audio cassettes that accompany textbooks. Then there are video cassettes that provide visual reinforcement and explanation of academic points. The radio has long since been used as a conveyer of information relevant to school children. Similarly, there are many TV programmes specially designed for learners to help them in understanding matters related to their school subjects.

In many cases, audio and video cassettes are considered suitable alternatives to print materials. In other words, the course is a combination of print, audio and video materials. It seems quite convincing that these three types of materials can supplement one another, and as a composite package, they can provide the most desirable learning opportunities to children. The production of such a package may be very costly, but that is not of immediate concern to us. The idea that teaching learning materials include books as well as other items remains valid. Think of very small children. They can't read books. Posters, charts, toy models, etc. are essential materials for them. Books prepared for them contain many pictures than words. When children are taken to a park to look at flowers and name them, to count trees and chase butterflies, the book of nature is being used as suitable instructional materials.

Textbooks have traditionally played a more perceptible role than other types of materials in our educational programmes, but they are by no means the only resource available to learners and teachers. An innovative teacher can harness almost anything to the task of effective teaching, and that item being to play the role of teaching materials. In language courses, listening and speaking skills are sought to be developed to the maximum. The textbook seems particularly inadequate for such tasks unless it is supplemented by listening and speaking opportunities. Audio materials, question answer sessions, debates, discussions and elocution contest can provide these opportunities. All these are broadly covered by the notion of teaching/learning materials and strategies.

To sum up, any material whether print or non-print that provides a learning opportunity consistent with the learner's age, aptitude and level will be considered learning and instructional material.

Usefulness of Instructional Material

Most teachers and learners, when asked this question, will instantly answer in affirmative: 'Yes, we do'. How else shall we ever teach a somewhat different view of the matter and feel reconciled to a teaching/learning situation even in the absence of prescribed materials. Theoretically, it is possible to teach or to learn without any given materials. But that is possible only in special cases with a small group of learners. The teacher will have to make special efforts to decide as to what to teach when, how and how much. Such a plan is unlikely to meet with success in situations where the number of learners is very large and the requirements of education are varied and complex. Besides, academic and pedagogic decisions are too important to be left to individual discretion. It is, therefore, desirable to agree to the view that specially designed materials are needed in a formal educational pattern. A textbook is necessary not only because it contains all the information required but also because it is a practical aid to the process of teaching and learning. The difference between a textbook and a general book on the same subject is merely this, that the former is meant for a particular group and provider provide specific information whose limits have been predetermined, whereas the latter is meant for a general group and seeks to cover a much wider range of information and knowledge. Given a particular level of learning, the course book defines the limits of its area and gives as much information as is considered essential to the target group. It is no longer the teacher's job to decide how much. It is all laid down in the book.

From the learner's point of view, the course book is important in that s/he can go back to it any number of times for reinforcement, clarification and a better understanding of the content. What is taught by the teacher may have been learnt at that time, but one might have difficulty later in recalling the matter in all its details. The textbook is there to be studied all over again.

The course book is also important because it gives us a chance to learn through reading, which is one of the major skills in the learning process. That is why it is recommended that one's reading should not be confined to the course books alone. One should begin with the prescribed book, and given interest and inclination, transcend it to acquire deeper knowledge of the subject. Children who have learnt to read with comprehension should be encouraged to read poems and stories outside the course materials. Wide reading enlarges one's scope of understanding and appreciation. The course book introduces us to the important skill of reading.

Q2. Delineate the base of material development.

Or

Why the task of material development needs special attention?

Ans. Course materials are important for both teachers and learners. The task of material development in different subject areas, thus, assumes special significance. It is a highly specialised job and should be undertaken by experts in the area after a lot of planning and reflection. The planning will take ahead. Who will do the job, how and under what time schedule? What will be the process of development and finalisation of materials? Are enough funds available for the task to be successfully completed on time? These are some basic questions, which are to be answered before planning. Then, there are academic issues like the requirements of a well considered policy on education and the guidelines laid down in the school curriculum (curriculum refers to a comprehensive statement about educational goals and objectives, process of teaching and learning, materials evaluation, teacher preparation, etc.) has a syllabus (a general statement about course content and specification) been prepared in the subject area. The learner's age, interests, level of proficiency, aptitude and personality are important consideration for the materials to become interesting and effective. The teacher's perceived style of functioning lecture method or interactive approach also plays an important role in the construction of course materials. What will be the size of the materials — a single book or a set of books with or without supplementary material? Are lessons to be new texts or texts selected, edited or rewritten? Will the proposed materials effect a smooth transition from the previous level and lead on naturally to the next? These are some academic and pedagogic questions that need to be carefully sorted out before the task of materials construction is undertaken.

Let us now be a little more specific about some academic issues. Take the case of a course book in English for class VI. We are one of the course writers. Assume that the practical aspects of management and administration have already been taken care of. What are some of the questions we would want to ask before starting work? Consider, the following questions and the ideas that they evoke:

- Is a syllabus in English available? We need to study the teaching items specified in the syllabus. Are we teaching isolated sentences or short but connected texts? Are our texts appropriate to the social settings? Are we teaching them all the skills?
- Why are we teaching English to our students? Surely, it serves some important social and cultural functions. It prepares them for higher education in areas where knowledge is not available in our own languages. It has a rich literary tradition. It is a world language. It is the associate official language in our country. English, therefore, should be taught. Hence, there is a need for good textbook.

- What about the socio-cultural milieu of the book? If it is meant for children living in villages and small towns, there should be references to the surroundings they are familiar with, the clothes they wear, and so on.
- Is English introduced everywhere at the Primary level or after class V? We know that in most parts of the country it is introduced in schools from class VI as a second language. There are also many schools everywhere which start English in Class I. We are now thinking of a book which will be used in the first year of the English teaching programme. In other words, Class VI will be Class I as far as English is concerned. Then why can't we use the Class I book here? Certainly not, because the age and mental level and interests of the learners are different at this level. We start from scratch but provide textual matter that will appeal to ten year old children. Situations presented in the lessons will be substantially different.
- Are we producing only one textbook in English? This seems reasonable during the first year of learning English. Since children haven't learnt to read with ease yet, there is no point in giving them supplementary reading material. How are we developing their listening skills and improving their ability to learn a new sound system? An audio cassette should accompany the textbook. That will be of great help.
- What should be the level of language and presentation? The course book should not begin with connected texts. Let us follow the principle of progressive movement from simple to complex to more complex. They should learn a certain number of words and phrases and should be able to write short and connected sentences at the end of the course.

One can think of many other areas of academic interest as well. These are only sample questions and their tentative answer hinting at the type of preparation necessary before the course book is actually designed. Similar reflections in other subject areas will be necessary for a complete set of materials to be used at a given level.

Q3. What are the features of course materials?

Ans. Course materials are used by teachers and learners, and very often learning is confined only to the information contained in them. Many teachers are unfortunately in a hurry of finish the prescribed course to ensure good results, and in the process neglect crucial methods and strategies through which information can be better assimilated by learners. Learners also study the materials with an eye on the final examination, and in a process deny themselves the pleasure that acquisition of knowledge through wider reading and understanding may bring. This is the bane of all routine teaching and learning. Innovative teachers and careful learners can surely work together to put the course materials to better use by treating them as mere starting points on the road to knowledge, leading to new pathways and avenues through a process of search and discovery. The teaching item prescribed has to be learnt, but the knowledge, thus, acquired should be applied to situations and settings outside the course books. The learning of different tense forms, their structure and use, in English is an important teaching item and has to be mastered. But having learnt it, the learner motivated to use this knowledge in his/her responses to real life situations. In other words, is s/he merely writing correct sentences in simple past tense, or is s/he also using this tense form correctly in describing an actual visit to a neighbouring town in the recent past. This is possible by exploiting the prescribed materials to the maximum on the one hand, and supplementing them by task and activities not necessarily prescribed on the other. This is also possible by evaluating materials from time to time and revising and updating them to fill the gaps wherever necessary.

- A teacher or evaluator should ask whether the book covers all the content specifications as given in the syllabus. Is the book based on the syllabus which is a general statement of the pedagogical arrangement of learning content? If not, it is inadequate. This inadequacy, if it exists, will seriously interfere with the learner's movement to the next higher stage. A gap will remain between Class VI and Class VII in terms of expected learning outcomes. The learner will have difficulty in coping with the content of Class VII book. The book should be in accordance with the exiting syllabus in terms of coverage.
- The book should reflect a view of the learner for whom it is intended, i.e. age and interests (topics chosen and types of learning activity, such as suitability of role-play and other tasks), level of proficiency in English (first, second or third year of English and scope for catering to a group of mixed proficiency) and learning style and personality (problem solving or rote learning or both, interactive classroom or studying alone).
- A language course book should also reflect a view of the language learning process whether language is perceived as a set of structures and in effect, a sum total of its discrete parts, or whether it is essential for communication and takes into account communicative acts in the context of socially appropriate settings. Does form get precedence over meaning or vice versa? The design of the book, its exercises and takes, will approximate to the authors' view of language learning.
- The book should reflect the relative emphasis laid on separate language abilities, i.e. reading/writing/listening/speaking. Which skills are likely to be more functional in the larger

perspective? Do our students need to read and write more than speak and listen through the medium of English, or is the situation reverse/different? That will depend upon the functions English is expected to perform in our social, culture and academic life.

- Does the book reflect in a serious manner the value system of the community for which it is intended? The content/text is a sensitive carrier of desired values and attitudes to be inculcated among learners. A book that makes no reference to our festivals, national heroes, culture heritage and immediate past and present will have little or no cultural value to the learners.
- What type of questions and exercises, tasks and activities are given in the book? That will provide a clue to the final evaluation. The materials should reflect the type of examination that will follow the completion of the course.

Q4. What are the various types of syllabus?

Or

How is skill based syllabus different from a functional syllabus? [Dec-2010, Q.No.-3]

Ans. There are following types of syllabus:

(1) Situational Syllabus

With this type of syllabus, the essential component of organisation is a non-linguistic category, i.e. the situation. The underlying premise is that language is related to the situational contexts in which it occurs. The designer of a situational syllabus tries to predict those situations in which the learner will find him/herself, and applies these situations, for instance; seeing the dentist, going to the cinema and meeting a new student, as a basis for selecting and presenting language content. The content of language teaching is a collection of real or imaginary situations in which language occurs or is used. A situation usually includes several participants who are involved in some activity in a particular setting. The language used in the situation comprises a number of functions combined into a plausible part of available discourse. The main principle of a situational language teaching syllabus is to teach the language that occurs in the situations. In this syllabus, situational needs are important rather than grammatical units. The major organising feature is a list of situations which reflects the way language and behaviour are used everyday outside the classroom. Thus, by connecting structural theory to situations, the learner is able to induce the meaning from a relevant context. One advantage of the situational approach is that motivation will be heightened since it is "learner centered rather than subject centered".

(2) Skill-based Syllabus

Skills are abilities that people must be able to do to be competent enough in a language, rather independently of the situation or context in which the language use can occur. In this syllabus, the content of the language teaching involves a collection of particular skills that may play a role in using language. Although situational syllabuses combine functions together into specific settings of language use, skill-based syllabi merge linguistic competencies (pronunciation, vocabulary, grammar and discourse) together into generalised types of behaviour, such as listening to spoken language for the main idea, writing well-formed paragraphs, delivering effective lectures, and so forth. The chief rationale behind skill-based instruction is to learn the specific language skill. Another less important objective might be to develop more general competence in the language, learning only incidentally any information that may be available while utilising the language skills. Such a syllabus will contain a list of items as given below:

- Making notes from a talk
- making notes from a book
- reading for primary information
- reading intensively
- using a dictionary or a source book
- writing an essay, a paragraph or a notice.

Notice that, though each item concentrates on a given skill, every item subsumes other skills too. 'Making notes' seems like a combination of Listening comprehension and writing ability. Reading for 'primary information' is likewise a combination of reading with speed and (mental) note making. It presupposes the ability to make notes.

(3) Grammatical or Structural Syllabus

This is recognised as the traditional syllabus which is often organised along grammatical lines giving primacy to language form. The focus is on the outcomes or the product. It is, in fact, a grammatical syllabus in which the selection and grading of the content is on the basis of the complexity and simplicity of grammatical items. In other words, it specifies structural patterns as the basic units of learning and organises these according to such criteria as structural complexity, difficulty, regularity, utility and frequency. The learner is expected to master each structural step and add it to his/her grammar collection. It makes ample use of highly controlled, tightly structured and sequenced pattern practice drills.

(4) Functional Syllabus

The chief emphasis of this syllabus is upon the communicative purpose and conceptual meaning of language, i.e. *notions* and *functions*. In other words, the content of the language teaching is a number of the *functions* that are performed on using the language, or of the *notions* that language is utilised to express. Functions can be exemplified by instances such as inviting, requesting, agreeing, apologising and notions embrace age, colour, size, comparison, time, etc. Besides, grammatical items, situational elements are considered at subsidiary level of importance. As opposed to the hypothesis of structural and situational syllabuses which lies in the fact that it is most often in search of 'how' or 'when' and 'where' the language, the functional syllabus seeks for 'what is a learner communicates through language'. An important point regarding functional syllabus is that the needs of the students have to be explored and analysed by different types of interaction and communication a learner may be involved in. Accordingly, needs analysis is central to the design of functional syllabuses. Needs analysis should be taken into account so as to establish the necessary objectives. Apart from needs, analysis that has an implicit focus on the learner, this type of syllabus proposes a new list consisting of notions and functions that become the main focus in a syllabus.

(5) Topic-based Syllabus

It is referred to as topic-based syllabus uses topics/themes as its starting point. Topics, like titles of textual pieces in any course book, range from the weather to smoking to space travel, the focus being thematic content rather than structural items.

Q5. What are the basic requirements of the communicative approach in terms of materials, methods and classroom management? What are the advantages?

Or

Mention the features of the Communicative Approach. How does it aid in language learning?

Ans. The communicative approach is based on the idea that learning language successfully comes through having to communicate real meaning. When learners are involved in real communication, their natural strategies for language acquisition will be used, and this will allow them to learn how to use the language. Practicing question forms by asking learners to find out personal information about their colleagues is an example of the communicative approach, as it involves meaningful communication.

There is no basic conflict between communicative competence and linguistic competence. In fact, the former is a product of a combination of 'grammatical competence' and what is referred to as 'sociolinguistic competence'. Grammatical competence refers to the mastery of the grammatical rules and structures of the language. It is essential to understand the literal meaning of sentences and texts. 'Sociolinguistic competence' refers to the ability to understand the appropriateness of the social context in which utterances are produced and exchanged. It also involves the ability to produce and exchange. It also involves the ability to produce socially appropriate utterances. Such an ability would take into account features like social conventions, degree of intimacy/formality, status and role of speakers/listeners and the overall purpose of the utterances. It is not difficult to come across utterances that are linguistically perfect but contextually inadequate or even offensive. It would seem that a functional approach to language teaching concerns itself with meaning and contextual appropriacy as well as with grammatical form, thought the emphasis is far greater on the former. As a result, it is inclined towards fluency (sustained participation) and not merely towards accuracy (grammatical correctness). Using language in socially appropriate and well-defined contexts is more important than doing exercises on language. Likewise, learner participation in classroom interaction plays a more dominant role than teacher-centred instruction. The teacher is viewed as a facilitator of learning and the learner becomes an active participant in activities involving discussion, role-play and sorting out differences of opinions in academic matters.

Materials produced on the basis of the communicative criteria list language functions and corresponding grammatical forms for the performance of those functions. Topic-based pieces, dialogues and other simplified text are then followed by tasks and activities in place of the conventional types of exercises such as lists of difficult words and their meanings, or substitution tables.

The classroom seating arrangement, in ideal conditions, is also different from that of a conventional classroom. Learners are expected to form themselves into small groups and move around freely whenever necessary. The new seating arrangement is a replica of a real-world situation in which spontaneity is ranked higher than cold formality. The grammatical approach dominated the ELT scene till the early-1970s when it became apparent that it was not enough for learners to be 'structurally competent' but 'communicatively deficient'. The ability to produce or write correct sentences, was generally felt necessary but not sufficient. This dissatisfaction with the 'product' of ELT programmes led to a debate which culminated in the development and adoption of the new approach in a big way. Materials were prepared according to communicative criteria and methods/techniques were reshaped according to the requirements of the new approach. One positive contribution of the new movement is a fairly comprehensive perspective in which language teaching and learning has come to be viewed in recent years. This new approach has provided fresh insights into syllabus construction, materials development and classroom methodology. Terms like 'communication', 'real-life', 'functions', 'appropriacy', 'context' and 'discourse' have gained common currency and the teacher has often felt obliged to introspect over his/her new role. To that extent, the approach has been useful, thought to what extent it has brought about concrete gains in language education is still far from clear.

Following are the some features of communicative approach:

- An emphasis on learning to communicate through interaction in the target language.
- The introduction of authentic texts into the learning situation.

- The provision of opportunities for learners to focus, not only on the language but also on the learning process itself.
- An enhancement of the learner's own personal experiences as important contributing elements to classroom learning.
- An attempt to link classroom language learning with language activation outside the classroom.

Q6. How would you evaluate materials to decide whether they are suitable for your learners? Explain both the kinds of evaluation.

Or

If you were to do an internal evaluation of a course book prescribed for your students what areas will you focus on? Give examples.

[June-2011, Q.No.-5]

Or

'Evaluation of materials is an interesting and useful exercise for all teachers'. Do you agree? Give reasons. What does of an ELT course book would you look at when you are evaluating materials externally?

[Dec-2010, Q.No.-5]

Or

Discuss the role of a teacher in adaptation of teaching materials to suit the needs of the learners. Provide an example from your textbook where in you adapted the material for your learners.

[Dec-2012, Q.No.-5]

Ans. Material evaluation is an important part of the professional activity of a teacher. The process of evaluation involves measuring the suitability of a given set of materials to the stated objectives of a teaching programme. If the main objective of a short term language course is the development of reading ability and the course book inappropriate for the course. This is not to suggest that the book is of a poor quality in every respect, only that it does not match up to the objectives of the teaching programme. On the other hand, a book which seems appropriate to being with, may turn out to be a partial failure in actual use. Or take a book which at first glance appears not user friendly, but eventually proves to be really useful in a practical sense. Evaluation, thus, is an on-going process. It is not an impulsive one time 'value judgement' but rather an act of slow trialing to discover the extent to which the material can act as an effective resource for teaching and learning.

External Evaluation

It is natural for a teacher to want to know 'something' about the books(s) s/he is asked to teach to a group of children. The cover, the table of contents, the blurb and particularly the introduction will yield bits of information about the contents of the book and the purpose for which it has been written. The preliminary overview of material by teachers is the external evaluation of course books. Theoretically, it is possible for teachers to form a fairly reliable opinion of the materials open to selection, and decide which book(s) can be gainfully used for a particular teaching programme. The organisation of material is indicated explicitly in the table of contents. The blurb as well as the introduction provides a clear picture of the plan and objectives of the materials. Who is it intended for? What does it seek to achieve and how? In what way is it an improvement on other materials available in the market? Some of the claims made in 'introductions' will read as follows:

- This book provides a teaching-learning package which should enable the learner to employ the language s/he is learning in the most optimal way possible to build further competencies.
- This book exposes the learner to a variety of authentic written language. It gives them confidence in coping with it. There are multiple opportunities here for oral fluency and language use.
- There are samples of functional language, which cause problems to learners. This book provides excellent opportunities for practicing language in actual use.
- Here is a wide thematic range, likely to interest and motivate the average learner. All the themes are generative in terms of useful vocabulary areas.

Notice that the claims made above are fairly strong, and need careful evaluation in order to see if they are justified. The justification will lie in the manner in which content has been organised and presented into teachable units.

From the introduction and the table of contents, one can obtain information regarding the following points:

- What is the target group?
- What is their proficiency level? Are they beginners, or intermediate level learners or adult learners?
- What is the context in which the material is to be used? Is it a general teaching programme or a specific course focussing only on some aspects of language use?
- How have units/lessons been organised? How many lessons intended for how many teaching hours? How has the language been presented?
- What is the writer's view of language learning and teaching methodology?
- Are there pictures, charts, diagrams? How closely are they integrated into the text?
- Is the text too culturally loaded for the learner to understand it?
- Is the material subversive of gender equality, peace and human rights? In other words, what is the value of system presented explicitly or implicitly?

The external evaluation or the preliminary overview of the course books is an important step in the process of assessing their appropriateness for adoption/selection. If they are, thus, found to be potentially useful, one can continue with a more detailed or 'internal' evaluation.

Internal Evaluation

Internal evaluation refers to an 'in depth' investigation of the materials to find out how far the claims made by publishers/authors are justified and whether those claims have been adequately translated into content. External evaluation provides the proper background for internal evaluation. It is not enough to state that the four language skills have been sought to be developed in this book (the introduction has made that claim). Has the writer actually covered all the language skills in a balanced, integrated manner? Is the integration natural so as to be appropriate to the context in which the curriculum requires us to teach them? In the treatment of skills, has the author confined himself/herself to isolated sentences or has s/he gone beyond them to include extended text for the reading ability to develop? Thus, in checking the truth and justification of the writer's claims, internal inspection will consist in examining the following in particular:

- The presentation of the skills in the course materials.
- The grading and sequencing of the materials. Most materials do not have any marked grading. Grading refers to the principle of moving from simple to complex in such a manner that the learner finds the upward movement both challenging and rewarding. The grading and sequencing of items/units is an important consideration in assessing the overall adequacy of the materials.
- The nature of the text. Is it mainly in the form of sentences or very short paragraphs or extended reading passages?
- If development of listening skills is one of the claims made, is the book accompanied by audio material? For a variety of reasons, recorded materials do not find a place in our language courses. Natural and spontaneous speech/dialogue on types is essential for developing listening skills. Teachers own speech may not be good or adequate materials for listening exercises.
- Are there dialogues in the materials for developing skills? How natural/artificial are those dialogues? Are these opportunities for learners to learn to speak in the manner that makes foe natural interaction?
- Exercises, tests and other practice material. To what extent do exercises reflect learner's needs?
- Teacher-learner balance in the use of materials. Some materials may be good for teachers thought not equally friendly for the

learners. Is there provision for self-study? Do the materials promote the relationship that exists or should exist, between the teacher and the learner?

Q7. If asked to select a textbook for your learners, what would be the criteria for your choice?

Or

What do you understand by the term 'adapting materials'? Why does a classroom teacher need to adapt the material in the textbook?

[June-2012, Q.No.-2]

Or

How would you adopt materials for your learners? Mention the points you will keep in mind.

Ans. Evaluation leads to 'adoption' of materials. The fact of adoption by no means guarantees the ultimate success in the use of materials. Those who deal with the materials (teachers and learners) are better qualified than others to pronounce judgment on the initial selection and say how with a little 'adaptation' the same materials can be more meaningfully used. Adaptation, thus, is a process dependent upon and subsequent to the process of adoption. It involves consideration of possible changes that have to be made in the materials so that they can be worked with in a balanced way according to the objectives of a specific teaching situation. The changes can be effected in terms of deleting or adding portions; modifying, simplifying or reordering parts so that the materials can match up to the needs, expectations and proficiency level of learners. Evaluating and adapting of materials are very important. Why should adaptation, on the spot adjustment or a formal reformulation leading to rewriting or revision, be necessary at all? Think of probable situations when the material does not lend itself to effective implementation. Here are some examples:

- A reading passage containing too many new and different vocabulary items. What is to be done? Select a small number of new words and explain each of them. Teach new words. Let children have an alternative passage. Simplify the passage using only a limited number of new words. Here is a wide range of possibilities, but in each case 'adaptation' in one form or another seems necessary.
- There is no grammar to plenty of it, at the end of a lesson. Some grammar points have not been adequately exemplified.
- Comprehension questions are too simple, or too few, and the ones given test only factual comprehension without real understanding.
- The subject matter of some passage is inappropriate to the intellectual level of the group. Should those passages be deleted or modified?
- There is unsuitable cultural loading of the content and children should not be exposed to it. If instances of this nature are too

many, the entire book may have to be replaced.

- The size of the material is unmanageable in the time available.
- There is no variety in the exercises and activities and classroom interaction remains dull and uninspiring.

The above possibilities cover crucial aspects of language use, skills and classroom management and interaction. How are the situations to be remedies? The remedy lies, one hopes, in the techniques applied to content to bring about changes in it. Some changes can be made by 'personalising', 'individualising' or 'localising' the content. 'Personalising' the content refers to increasing its relevance in relation to the learner's interests and educational needs. 'Individualising' the content refers to bringing it in line with learner's style of learning, both individually (wherever possible) and collectively. 'Localising' the content implies lending it a touch of 'logical colour' or making it appear familiar in relation to the cultural as well as geographical features of the region. Then there are other techniques/ procedures that can be used to change the content according to one's requirements. The techniques can be used once at a time or in combination with one another depending upon the changed required. Consider the following in particular:

Adding: Adding implies supplying some more exercises for better exemplification. At the end of every text, for instance, there is a set of five or six comprehension questions. The teacher can supply many more keeping in mind the time schedule. The teacher, thus, is adding to the given quantity of content by extending it. It is also possible to expand the content by adding qualitatively different portions. The teacher can innovate by asking new questions to test the learner's understanding of the text beyond factual details. Another example of adding can be a supplementary reading passage to reinforce the teaching points of the given passage, or some new exercise to explain a point of grammar. Teachers adopt this procedure of 'adding' almost all the time. They supplement the material while dealing with a given text, or introduce items through an introductory session before taking up the lesson as such.

Deleting: Deleting or omitting is the opposite of adding or extending. Instead of putting in more, something is taken out of the content because it is repetitive, not quite appropriate or simply too elaborate. If there are too many exercises of the same type, only a few can be attempted leaving the rest in favour of a new teaching item. Deleting and adding often go together. The purpose of both is to adjust the content to the academic needs of the learner.

Modifying: Modifying the content is to introduce 'internal' changes in it, like changing the focus of an exercise or text by means of rewriting parts of it or restructuring the class management. Modifying is much more than simple adding or deleting in qualitative terms. Changing a reading passage into dialogue form (involving restructuring classroom management), or turning a written exercise into an oral one, deliberately taking into account aspects of speaking ability are examples of modifying the content. This procedure needs greater care and planning because it implies an 'internal' change — a change in approach and focus of a piece of material.

Simplifying: Simplification is something that happens, or many happen, in every classroom when teachers and learners are working with the materials. Simplification refers to the act of making items-instructions, explanations, questions, texts appear simpler than they are in the original. In the initial years of schooling, children can't read much. Instructions to learners in the textbook/workbook are in fact addressed more to teachers than to learners. Instructions are re-worded or explained through gestures/actions by the teacher. Similarly, sentences in isolation or connected texts can also be simplified, simplifying a text often implies rewriting it. Courses contain simplified texts, but if they don't match closely to the proficiency level of the learner, they can be further simplified, if not rewritten altogether. Texts can be simplified in terms of (i) sentence structure (reducing length of sentences and changing complex sentenced into simple ones), (ii) lexical content (controlled vocabulary), and (iii) grammatical structure (changing passive into active, past tense into present tense and indirect speech into direct speech). Simplification also consists in changing the design and layout of the text. For instance, a large piece can be broken up into smaller units and each unit is taken up separately with built-in linkages with the units that follow. Simplifying a text often result in changing the stylistic effect of that text, especially a literary text, as well as the intention of the writer. But that is a risk worth taking in the interest of better communication and learning.

Reordering: Reordering means 're-working' of a course book by changing the sequence of its units, or changing the sequence of presentation within a single unit. This is not always necessary, if the materials have been subjected to careful inspection before adoption. However, the need for presenting the content in a different order may arise if the teacher finds that working through from beginning to end is neither possible nor desirable. It may not be possible due to time constraint, and not desirable due to the existing proficiency level of the group. Pieces can be grouped in a new order according to their thematic or linguistic similarities. If there are two nature poems in the course book, the teacher may decide to take them up in succession treating them as complementary to each other. Limited reordering within a single unit, if not through the whole book, may be tried as an experimental activity.

Adapting materials through adding, deleting or simplifying is of great practical value because it makes the content more relevant to the learners. Evaluation and adaptation of materials are supportive of each other and both develop from an understanding of the adaptation of materials are supportive of each other and both develop from an understanding of the features of the syllabus and the organisational principles of materials.

Question Papers

TEACHING STRATEGIES: CTE-03
December, 2010

*Note: Attempt all questions. All questions carry **equal** marks.*

Q1. Write short notes on *any four* of the following. Give examples wherever necessary.

(a) Teacher as resource.

Ans. Refer to Chapter-1, Q.No.-6

(b) Fixed pairs and flexible pairs in pair work activities.

Ans. Refer to Chapter-1, Q.No.-3

(c) Three phases of a listening lesson.

Ans. Refer to Chapter-2, Q. No.-8

(d) Factors leading to inattentiveness in an English class.

Ans. Refer to Chapter-1, Q.No.-7

(e) Prediction in reading comprehension.

Ans. Refer to Chapter-2, Q.No.-1

(f) Teaching pronunciation.

Ans. Refer to Chapter-3, Q.No.-7

Q2. What are teacher's beliefs and attitudes about language learning? How can they be overcome?

Ans. Refer to Chapter-1, Q.No.-9

Or

Do you agree with this statement, Many discipline problems arise due to the teacher herself?

Give examples of ways in which a teacher herself is responsible for indiscipline in the class. What should she do to ensure smooth teaching-learning?

Ans. Refer to Chapter-1, Q.No.-7 and Q.No.-8

Q3. What are the advantages of organising pair/groupwork in teaching?

Give an example from your own teaching experience where group/ pair work was organised successfully to develop learner's skills.

Ans. Refer to Chapter-1, Q.No.-3

Or

'Many teachers hesitate to organise group work in their teaching'. Why?

What are the advantages of organising group work?

Ans. Refer to Chapter-1, Q.No.-3 and Q.No.-4

Q4. 'Spoken and written language are used for the purpose of communicating with others; They are similar yet different. Do you agree?

Explain the similarities and differences between the two.

Ans. Refer to Chapter-3, Q.No.-1and Q.No.-2

Or

What, according to you, should be emphasised when you are teaching students, how to speak with fluency or accuracy? Give reasons for your answer.

Ans. Refer to Chapter-3, Q.No.-7

Q5. Which is the best approach/es to the teaching of grammar? Why? What are the steps you take to teach a grammar lesson effectively?

Ans. Refer to Chapter-3, Q. No.-16

Or

Evaluation of materials is an interesting and useful exercise for all teachers. Do you agree? Give reasons.
What areas of an ELT course book would you look at when you are evaluating materials externally?

Ans. Refer to Chapter-4, Q.No.-6

◈◈◈

"Don't aim for success if you want it; just do what you love and believe in, and it will come naturally."

TEACHING STRATEGIES: CTE-03
June, 2011

Note: Attempt all questions. All questions carry ***equal*** *marks.*

Q1. Write short notes on *any four* of the following. Give examples wherever necessary.

(a) Pair work and Group work

Ans. Refer to Chapter-1, Q.No.-3

(b) Dealing with indiscipline students in an English class.

Ans. Refer to Chapter-1, Q.No.-8

(c) Role of the teacher in a communicative class.

Ans. Refer to Chapter-3, Q.No.-12

(d) Silent Vs loud reading.

Ans. Refer to Chapter-2, Q.No.-9

(e) Extensive listening and intensive listening.

Ans. Refer to Chapter-2, Q.No.-6

(f) Problems faced by learners in writing.

Ans. Though the teaching of writing seems to be highly desirable, teachers often question the extent to which it may be feasible in our context. There are numerous problems in our context which work against the teaching of writing. The three perspectives of it are the learner, the teacher and the administrator. The learners are unmotivated; they consider the composition classes as meaningless and irrelevant. According to them, these classes do not help them in any way in preparing for the examination. Given the choice, they would prepare to spend the time more 'usefully' in memorising summaries from guide books. They find no thrill in writing; for them the teacher is the only intended reader, whose sole joy seems to lie in a liberal use of red ink to underline mistakes. If writing is boring, receiving the evaluated scripts is frustrating and stifles whatever enthusiasm may be left. Most teachers have had no training in communicating through writing; they feel insecure in trying out new techniques. Further, the English syllabus is so heavy that in their eagerness to 'cover' the portions, they are forced to convert 'composition' classes into Prose and Poetry classes. Even those teachers who continue to teach composition in spite of all odds, find timely evaluation of scripts very difficult. With the large classes consisting ***of*** nearly hundred students, it becomes humanly impossible to do justice to evaluation. They are hence, forced to take the easy option of not making students write. The problems of learners and teachers are further aggravated by the administrators who impose their own peculiar, outdated notions on them. They insist on weekly exercises, underlining of all the mistakes, absolute silence in the classrooms, etc. Innovative teachers are prevented from trying out new approaches.

These problems, however, are not insurmountable. Current research in writing has explored learner-oriented approaches to writing. Teacher-orientation programmes may be organised to make teachers more positive. And once teachers and learners join hands, they could easily convince administrators.

Q2. What is practitioner research? Why should teachers be encouraged to have a questioning altitude to their own teaching, and be research minded?

Ans. Refer to Chapter-1, Q.No.-10 and Q.No.-11

Or

How can teachers monitor their own classroom teaching? What aspects of your own teaching - learning should you monitor as a teacher?

Ans. Refer to Chapter-1, Q.No.-9

Q3. What are the characteristics of reading? What do you understand by 'an efficient reader'?

Ans. Refer to Chapter-2, Q.No.-10

Or

What are the enabling skills that can help students to become good readers? What are the problems that readers generally face when they engage with a text?

Ans. Refer to Chapter-2, Q.No.-1 and Q.No.-11

Q4. With practical examples show how you would use the following approaches to teaching grammar:

(a) teaching grammar in context and

(b) teaching grammar as discourse.

Ans. Refer to Chapter-3, Q.No.-18

Or

What should be emphasised when you are teaching your students how to speak fluency or accuracy? Give reasons for your belief. Give examples of classroom activities you use to develop fluency and accuracy in your students.

Ans. Refer to Dec-2010, Q.No.-4

Q5. How can you use language games successfully in a communicative classroom? Give examples of some language games you have used with your students.

Ans. Refer to Chapter-3, Q.No.-8

Or

If you were to do an internal evaluation of a course book prescribed for your students what areas will you focus on? Give examples.

Ans. Refer to Chapter-4, Q.No.-6

TEACHING STRATEGIES: CTE-03
December, 2011

*Note: Attempt all questions. All questions carry **equal** marks.*

Q1. Write short notes on *any four* of the following: Give examples wherever necessary.

(a) Pair work and group work

Ans. Refer to June-2011, Q.No.-1(a)

(b) Direct approach to teaching the speaking skill.

Ans. Refer to Chapter-3, Q.No.-6

(c) Interactive approach to teaching writing

Ans. Refer to Chapter-3, Q.No.-15

(d) Teaching conversation skills

Ans. Refer to Chapter-2, Q.No.-6

(e) Developing instructional materials

Ans. Refer to Chapter-4, Q.No.-1

(f) 'Intensive' and 'extensive' reading.

Ans. Refer to Chapter-2, Q.No.-12

Q2. Show how you would use the following approaches to teaching grammar with the help of practical experiences:

(a) Teaching grammar in realistic situations

(b) Teaching grammar to enable communication.

Ans. Refer to June-2011, Q.No.-4

Or

Describe different activities you would organise to develop the sub-skills of reading comprehension of students. Give atleast four activities.

Ans. Refer to Chapter-2, Q.No.-1

Q3. How is a skill based syllabus different from a structural syllabus?

Give examples of classroom activities and processes used with each.

Which of the two is more successful in enabling development of language skills? Give reasons.

Ans. Refer to Chapter-4, Q.No.-4

The skill-based syllabus is more successful in enabling development of language skills. This is because skill-based syllabus makes students independent and they can perform according to their skills. A skill based syllabus concerns itself, more than anything else, with what learners do as listeners, speakers, readers and writers. It envisages activities concentrating on the promotion of language arts. It envisages activities concentrating on the promotion of language arts.

Or

Why do discipline problems occur in a class? How can a teacher deal with them?

Ans. Refer to Chapter-1, Q.No.-7 and Q.No.-8

Q4. Listening is a skill that is most neglected in a formal classroom. Do you agree? Why suggest ways to overcome this.

Ans. Yes, I am agree with the given statement as most of the teachers may neglect listening in a formal classroom. Teachers should not do this. As students or learners, prefer playful methods in their studies. Thus, the informal kind of talk by the teacher is an excellent way of presenting listening material in the class. It can be interpolated at any stage in the lesson, serving as a relaxing break from more intensive work. It is easy to listen to, since it is 'live' and 'personal'.

Now, Refer to Chapter-1, Q.No.-7

Or

What, according to you, are the problems faced by learners in writing?

How can you help your students become good writers? Give examples of steps taken by you.

Ans. Refer to June-2011, Q.No.-1(f) and Chapter-3, Q.No.-13

Q5. How can teachers monitor their own classroom teaching? What aspects of your own teaching -learning should you monitor as a teacher? How would you do that?

Ans. Refer to June-2011, Q.No.-2

Or

What is the role of language games in a communicative classroom? Give examples of language games you have used in your classroom successfully (any 3).

Ans. Refer to June-2011, Q.No.-5

◈◈◈

TEACHING STRATEGIES: CTE-03
June, 2012

Note: Attempt all questions. All questions carry ***equal*** *marks.*

Q1. Write short notes on *any four* of the following:

Give examples wherever necessary.

(a) Dealing with indisciplined students in a class.

Ans. Refer to June-2011, Q.No.-1(b)

(b) Role of the teacher in a communicative class.

Ans. Refer to June-2011, Q.No.-1(c)

(c) Need of Practitioner Research

Ans. Refer to Chapter-1, Q.No.-11

(d) Direct approach to teaching of conversation skills.

Ans. Refer to Dec-2011, Q.No.-1(b)

(e) Pair work and group work

Ans. Refer to Dec-2011, Q.No.-1(a)

(f) Warm up activities and ice breakers.

Ans. Refer to Chapter-3, Q.No.-10

Q2. Show how you would use the following approaches to teaching grammar: Give practical examples in support.

(a) Teaching grammar with focus on fluency first.

(b) Teaching grammar using real life situations.

Ans. Refer to Dec-2011, Q.No.-2

Or

What do you understand by the term 'adapting materials'? Why does a classroom teacher need to adapt the materials in the text book?

Ans. Refer to Chapter-4, Q.No.-7

Q3. What are the problems that students may encounter while reading? Describe the different strategies that learners need to read effectively.

Ans. Refer to Chapter-2, Q.No.-11

Or

Why do listening and speaking skills get neglected in the English classroom? Suggest ways in which you can overcome this?

Ans. Refer to Chapter-2, Q.No.-6 and Q.No.-2

Q4. What do you understand by the process approach to writing? How is it different from the other approaches? Give examples.

Ans. Refer to Chapter-3, Q.No.-14

Or

How is a skill based syllabus different from a functional syllabus? Give examples of classroom activities and processes used with each to develop language skills of students.

Ans. Refer to Dec-2011, Q.No.-3

Q5. Imagine you have conducted an experiment in your classroom to develop communication skills of your students. Describe the objective, topic/area, methodology, findings and follow up action taken by you.

Ans. Refer to Chapter-1, Q.No.-2

Or

What are the key features you need to keep in mind in order to plan a lesson for a particular level (Please mention the level)?

Attempt an outline of a lesson plan on any topic of your choice.

Ans. Refer to Chapter-1, Q.No.-1

Teaching English at the Junior Level

- *Understand English when spoken:* His standard of speech should approximate the native speaker's so that if a native speaker speaks English, which is not above his level, he should be able to understand it.
- Acquire reading ability and read the material that is appropriate for his level.
- Acquire a vocabulary, which though limited, is enough to help him in the use of the language that he makes.
- Have his aim fixed at the conversational English, as it is used in speech. Our purpose in the beginning should be to help the students in acquiring a command over spoken forms, colloquial or conversational English, rather than the textbook English.
- Make simple statements through English. He should be able to frame short, simple sentences to express himself through speech and writing.
- Speak with a pronunciation that is acceptable. He should acquire a command over the phonemes of the language and speak English with proper stress and intonation.

- Respond to short conversational questions and to ask questions himself.
- Write English legibly and coherently using proper punctuation and capitals where necessary with correct spellings.
- Use English when he has to respond to calls, requests, greetings, etc. when he has to do the same to others.

Teaching English at the Senior Level

- Students at the end of the secondary stage should be able to speak English fluently and accurately. Fluency implies acquisition of a reasonable standard in speech–habits, which means speaking with an acceptable pronunciation and intonation.
- They should be able to speak freely. They should think in English and speak it with ease and frequently.
- They should be able to talk in English and to express their ideas in English in classroom, at home and in society. They should be able to respond and react to situations actively and not remain just a passive listener.
- They should acquire the ability to understand the native speakers and also be able to respond to them.
- They should be able to compose freely and independently in speech and writing.
- They should be able to read books with understanding. They should also be able to read newspapers and periodicals.
- They should acquire a vocabulary of 2500 words approximately and that should include frequent and choicest English phrases and idioms.
- They should be able to use reference materials, i.e. encyclopaedia, dictionaries, reference books, etc. when they stand in need thereof.

-: LESSON PLAN :-

(1) General Objectives

- To enable the students to understand, write and speak English correctly.
- To develop communication skills of the students.
- To develop the vocabulary and language style.
- To enable them to get knowledge contained in the lesson.
- To inculcate creativity in students.

(2) Specific Objectives

- To enable the students to define prepositions and their use in their own words.
- To enable the students to learn about various kinds of preposition.

(3) Previous Knowledge

The students must have general familiarities with different parts of speech, i.e. nouns, pronouns, adjective, verb, adverb, etc.

(4) Teaching Aids

Blackboard, chalk, duster, pointer, etc.

(5) Introduction

Teacher's Question	Student's Answer
(i) What do you know about parts of speech?	(i) The parts of speech are noun, adjective, pronoun, verb, adverb, preposition, conjunction and interjection.
(ii) Good, define noun.	(ii) Word used as the name of a person, place, or thing.
(iii) Define pronoun.	(iii) Word that takes the place of a noun.
(iv) Well, tell me about adjectives.	(iv) A word or a phrase used with a noun or pronoun to describe or point out the person, animal, thing or place which the noun names or to tell the number of quantity.
(V) What do you know about verb?	(V) Word used to express an action or state.
(vi) Good, what do you know about adverb?	(vi) Word used to add something to the meaning of a verb, an adjective or another adverb.
(vii) Do you know about prepositions?	(vii)...

(6) Statement of topic

Now, teacher will announce the topic, "Today, I shall teach you about prepositions and its various kinds".

(7) Presentation

Teaching Step	Teacher's Activity	Student's Activity
Step I: Meaning of preposition	The teacher will write some sentences on the blackboard, which are as follows: (a) The rat jumped off the table. (b) He is fond of cold–drinks. (c) There is a buffalo in the garden. Further, s/he will ask the following questions: (a) Which parts of speech are in the words 'jumped' and 'table'? (b) Which word is presenting the relationship between verb and noun in sentence(a)? (c) Which parts of speech are in the words 'fond' and 'cold–drinks' in sentence (b)? (d) What is the function of 'of' in sentence (b)? (e) Which parts of speech are in the words buffalo and garden in sentence (c)? (f) Which word is showing relationship between 'buffalo' and 'garden'?	(a) Jumped: Verb Table: Noun (b) The word 'off'. (c) Fond: Adjective Cold–drinks: Noun (d) Shows relationship between noun and adjective. (e) Buffalo: Noun Garden: Noun (f) The word 'in'.
Generalisation	The words off, of, in are here used as prepositions. A preposition is a word placed before a noun or a pronoun to show in what relation the person or thing denoted by it stands in regarding to something else.	The students will carefully listen and note down in their notebooks.

Contd...

Contd...

Teaching Step	Teacher's Activity	Student's Activity
	(The word preposition means 'that which is placed before') It will be noticed that: In sentence (a), the preposition joins a noun to a verb. In sentence (b), the preposition joins a noun to an adjective. In sentence (c), the preposition joins a noun to a verb.	
Step II: Kinds of Prepositions	Prepositions are of five different kinds: (a) Simple prepositions (b) Compound prepositions (c) Double prepositions (d) Participle prepositions (e) Phrase prepositions	The students will note down in their notebooks.
Simple Preposition	Simple prepositions are words like in, on, at, about, over, under, off, of, for, to, etc. For example: (a) She sat on the sofa. (b) He is going to the market. (c) He fell off the ladder. (d) There is some water in the bottle. (e) She is about seven. (f) They sat around the table. (g) The cat was hiding under the bed.	The students will note down in their notebooks.
Compound Preposition	Compound prepositions are words like without, within, inside, outside, into, beneath, below, behind, between, etc. For example:	The students will note down in their notebooks.

Contd...

Contd...

Teaching Step	Teacher's Activity	Student's Activity
	(a) He fell into the river. (b) She sat between her kids. (c) He sat beside her. (d) There is nothing inside the jar. (e) The teacher stood behind the desk. (f) The boy ran across the road.	
Double prepositions	Double prepositions are words like outside of, out of, from behind, from beneath, etc. For example, (a) Suddenly, he emerged from behind the curtain. (b) He walked out of the compound.	The students will note down in their note-books.
Participle prepositions	Participle prepositions are words like concerning, notwithstanding, pending, considering, etc. For example: (a) There was little chance of success, notwithstanding they decided to go ahead. (b) You did the job well, considering your age and inexperience.	The students will note down in their note-books.
Phrase prepositions	Phrase prepositions are phrases like because of, by means of, with regard to, on behalf of, instead of, on account of, in opposition to, for the sake of, etc. For example:	The students will note down in their note-books.

Contd...

Contd...

Teaching Step	Teacher's Activity	Student's Activity
	(a) I am standing here on behalf of my friends and colleagues. (b) The match was cancelled because of the rain. (c) He succeeded by means of perseverance.	

(8) Evaluation

Name the prepositions in the following sentences and tell the word which each governs:

- The lion and the unicorn fought for the crown.
- She sat by the fire and told me a tale.
- A fair little girl sat under a tree.
- Humpty Dumpty sat on a wall.
- I can never return with my poor dog Tray.
- I tried to reason him out of his fears.

(9) Homework

- Define preposition with examples.
- Define the various types of prepositions with proper examples.

TEACHING STRATEGIES: CTE-03
December, 2012

*Note: Attempt all questions. All questions carry **equal** marks.*

Q1. Write short notes on *any four* of the following:

Give examples wherever necessary.

(a) Teacher's role in pair and group work

Ans. Refer to Chapter-1, Q.No.-3

(b) Reading aloud

Ans. Refer to Chapter-2, Q.No.-9

(c) Differences between spoken and written language.

Ans. Refer to Chapter-3, Q.No.-2

(d) Negotiating meaning in a conversation

Ans. Refer to Chapter-3, Q.No.-5

(e) Interactive Approach in writing

Ans. Refer to Dec-2011, Q.No.-1(c)

(f) Supplementary Reader

Ans. Refer to Chapter-2, Q.No.-10

Q2. Do you agree with the statement the co-operation and collaboration are the key words that make for an effective learning situation? Discuss with examples.

Ans. Refer to Chapter-1, Q.No.-3

Or

Describe the ways in which you can monitor your own performance as well as the performance of your learners? Explain with the help of a teaching-learning situation.

Ans. Refer to Chapter-1, Q.No.-9

Q3. Comprehension or interpretation in listening comprise processing of knowledge and information. Explain. Provide two brief examples of listening in real life where both these come into play.

Ans. Refer to Chapter-2, Q.No.-6

Or

"The meaning of a written text does not merely lie in it, waiting to be passively absorbed by the reader". Discuss with examples.

Ans. Refer to Chapter-2, Q.No.-9

Q4. What are the various ways in which you could create need for communication? Describe two language activities or games through which you would do so.

Ans. Refer to Chapter-3, Q.No.-8

Or

The art of writing differs from the craft of writing. Explain using the example of a writing task.

Ans. Refer to Chapter-3, Q.No.-13

Q5. What does teaching 'grammar in context' mean? Taking any grammar item from your school syllabus provide a plan of a grammar lesson to exemplify the approach.

Ans. Refer to Chapter-3, Q.No.-18

Or

Discuss the role of a teacher in adaptation of teaching materials to suit the needs of the learners. Provide an example from your text book where in you adapted the material for your learners.

Ans. Refer to Chapter-4, Q.No.-6

◈◈◈

"Doubt, of whatever kind, can be ended by action alone"

TEACHING STRATEGIES: CTE-03
June, 2013

Note: *Attempt all questions. All questions carry* ***equal*** *marks.*

Q1. Write short notes on any four of the following.

Give examples wherever necessary.

(a) Open ended of tasks in the English classroom

Ans. Refer to Chapter-1, Q.No.-1

(b) Strategies of Reading

Ans. Bender (2004) states that once children learn to decode alphabetical sounds, entire words and phrases may be read as a unit. The end result is a faster, better reader. When students do not have to spend as much time decoding each individual sound in a word, they can put more energy into becoming a fluent reader who is better able to understand the meaning of what is being read.

Bender (2004) offers four different tactics for developing reading fluency in the classroom. The first of these is student-adult reading. In this scenario, a student reads one-on-one with an adult partner. The adult first reads the text, and then the student reads the text. They continue until the student becomes fluent at the passage read.

The second tactic discussed by Bender (2004) is choral reading. This simply incorporates having the group of children read the passage together multiple times until fluency is achieved.

Next, Bender (2004) discusses tape-assisted reading. In this scenario, students read the material along with a taped version of the text. This is continued until fluency is reached.

The fourth tactic discussed by Bender (2004) is partner reading, in which students pair up and take turns reading aloud. Bender suggests that more fluent readers be paired with slower readers so that the students may provide assistance to each other.

(c) Characteristics of spoken language

Ans. Refer to Chapter-3, Q.No.-3

(d) Extensive and intensive listening comprehension

Ans. Refer to Chapter-2, Q.No.-6

(e) Grammar for Communication

Ans. Refer to Chapter-3, Q.No.-18

Q2. A collaborative classroom is interactive and creates ways for proactive learning. But in order to organise an effective collaborative class a teacher needs to overcome certain problems. Discuss what problems there might be and how a teacher can overcome them. Provide examples from your experiences.

Ans. When teachers and schools move from traditional to collaborative instruction, several important issues are likely to arise. They are important concerns for teachers, administrators, and parents.

Classroom Control: Collaborative classrooms tend to be noisier than traditional classrooms. This is a legitimate issue for a number of people. Some teachers believe that noisy classrooms indicate lack of discipline or teacher control. In such situations, they argue, students cannot learn.

Since, collaborative classrooms do not lack structure. Indeed, structure becomes critical. Students need opportunities to move about, talk, ask questions, and so on. Thus, we argue that the noise in a smoothly running collaborative classroom indicates that active learning is going on. However, students must be taught the parameters within which they make their choices. Rules and standards must be stressed from the beginning, probably before any collaboration is initiated and reviewed throughout a school year.

Preparation Time for Collaborative Learning: Teachers and administrators may believe that new lesson plans must be formed for these classrooms. To a certain extent, they are correct. But many teachers already have created engaging units and activities that are easily implemented in a collaborative classroom. Furthermore, teachers can begin slowly, making changes in one subject area or unit within a subject area, probably one they are already very comfortable teaching, and then add other subjects and units. Teachers can also share their plans with each other. Indeed, if we expect students to collaborate, we should encourage teachers to do the same! Principals and curriculum specialists can also collaborate with teachers to plan effective segments of instruction. Moreover, there is a trade-off between the extra planning time needed and benefits such as less time correcting lessons, increased student motivation, and fewer attendance and discipline problems.

Individual Differences Among Students: Many people will doubt that individual differences can be better addressed in collaborative classrooms than in traditional classrooms with homogeneous grouping.

A major question people have concerns the advantage collaboration affords gifted or high-achieving students. There are two tough issues here. First, many teachers do not believe that low-achieving students have to contribute much to the learning situation; in effect, that they have no prior experiences or knowledge of value. Second, teachers worry that high-achieving students will be held back.

In response to the first issue, many collaborative teachers have expressed surprise when seemingly less able or weak students had insights and ideas that went way beyond what teachers expected. Further, if each student contributes something, the pool of collective knowledge will indeed be rich. In answer to the second concern, high-achieving students gain much from their exposure to diverse experiences and also from peer tutoring (e.g., Johnson and Johnson, 1989). Also, students who may be high achieving in one area may need help in other areas.

Teachers and others also wonder whether shy students can fully participate in a classroom that depends so much on dialogue. We suggest that these students might feel more comfortable talking in small groups that share responsibility for learning. Furthermore, interaction between learners can happen in ways other than oral dialogue, for example, writing and art.

A related concern is that many schools are structured homogeneously so that an individual teacher cannot form heterogeneous groups without involving changes in the entire school. A whole class of "low" readers are taught by one teacher and "average" by another. High school tracks are even more systematically entrenched. Clearly, these practices are not conducive to collaborative learning and require system-wide restructuring. Individual teachers or groups of teachers can initiate dialogue on the problem, however.

Individual Responsibility for Learning: This concern is a difficult one to solve unless major changes in other areas of schooling are also undertaken. Students are used to being graded for individual work; parents expect to know how their students fare in school. School staff and state departments depend on traditional assessments. In collaborative classrooms, it is often difficult to assign individual grades. Some teachers give group grades, but many students and parents are uncomfortable with these.

Ideally, assessment practices should be changed so that they are consistent with collaboration, with a new view of learning and with a thinking curriculum. In the meantime, effective ways have been developed whereby individual students can be evaluated in collaborative classrooms. For example, David Johnson and Roger Johnson, as well as Robert Slavin, advise making individuals responsible for subtasks in group work and then determining both group and individual grades.

Conflict of Values: Susan Florio-Ruane has observed that many teachers do not feel comfortable allowing students to initiate dialogue, determine topics or explore perspectives other than the teachers. This reluctance conflicts with the way effective caregivers teach their children in the home. Florio-Ruane and others, such as Annemarie Palincsar, have found that teachers often have difficulty in helping students to construct meaning, especially linking the new information to the prior knowledge and culture of the students. In part, this is because many teachers believe that their role is to transmit knowledge; in part, it is because they are held accountable for teaching discrete skills. In one poignant example, a student teacher's concern for grammar and punctuation prevented her from seeing the sophistication and meaning in what the child was actually communicating in a book report.

The reluctance people feel when asked to make major changes in the way they do things is clearly the most serious issue of those discussed here. Hardly a person exists who eagerly gives up familiar ways of behaving to attempt something that is unknown and is likely to have many challenges of implementation.

This problem requires leadership, support, and time to address. Staff development needs to address teachers' concerns.

Or

Action research by the practitioner is the most meaningful and effective research in the classroom. Discuss.

Give examples of any research that you might have undertaken during your career as a teacher.

Ans. Refer to Chapter-1, Q.No.-10

Action Research in an ESL Classroom: An example of using drawings to understand second language learners' prior learning experiences. The example also includes the use of student writing and interviewing to support the research.

Action Research about Science Experiences: In this example of action research, drawings, along with other data sources, are used to study students' experiences with science outside of the classroom context.

Q3. What are the different listening skills that can be exercised in the language class? Provide examples of listening tasks that you can organise in your classroom.

Ans. Refer to Chapter-2, Q.No.-1, Q.No.-2

Or

In what sense is reading called a psycholinguistic guessing game? Explain mentioning the knowledge and skills one requires to arrive at the meaning of a text.

Ans. Refer to Chapter-3, Q.No.-1, Q.No.-19

Q4. An efficient speaker of language needs much more than vocabulary, pronunciation and grammar of the language. Do you agree? Discuss, provide examples of activities that you would organise to develop the necessary skills.

Ans. Refer to Chapter-3, Q.No.-5

Or

What does the process oriented approach to writing comprise? Explain with the help of an example of a writing task.

Ans. Refer to Chapter-3, Q.No.-14

Q5. If you were asked to select textual teaching material for your class, what aspects would you look for? Discuss giving examples.

Ans. Refer to Chapter-4, Q.No.-7

Or

Is it realistic to exclude grammar from the communicative classroom? Why/Why not? Discuss.

Ans. Refer to Chapter-3, Q. No.-17

◈◈◈

TEACHING STRATEGIES: CTE-03
December, 2013

Note: Attempt all questions. All questions carry ***equal*** *marks.*

Q1. **Write short notes on any four of the following:**

(a) Role of the teacher in organising collaborative activities.

(b) Enabling skills for Listening and Reading

(c) The role of schemata in reading

(d) Spoken interaction; its characteristics

(e) Adapting materials

(f) The craft of writing

Q2. What are the different ways in which you can promote interaction in the classroom? Provide and discuss an example in steps to show how it aids learning.

Or

What are the different types of listening skills? Give examples of activities to support your answer.

Q3. It is said that the meaning of a written text is created collaboratively by the writer and the reader. Explain.

Or

What is the place of speaking in a communicative classroom? Give examples of ways in which you will create a need to communicate.

Q4. What do you understand by the process approach to writing? Give a brief plan of a process writing activity in the classroom.

Or

What are the key features of the typical language classroom? How does it differ from a content-based lesson?

Q5. What are the major kinds of syllabi that can be used for teaching English? Critically evaluate the syllabus you follow in the classroom in the light of the above.

Or

How will you decide whether the materials that you use in the classroom are suitable for a target group? Discuss the different means of evaluating such materials?

TEACHING STRATEGIES: CTE-03

June, 2014

*Note: Answer all questions. All question carry **equal** marks.*

Q1. Write short notes on any four of the following:

(a) The need for practitioner research

(b) Comprehension or interpretation in listening

(c) Faulty reading habits

(d) Communication Games

(e) Importance of textbooks in the Indian context.

(f) The need for teaching grammar in the classroom.

Q2. How has the role of the teacher changed? Provide an example to show how a teacher can become a collaborator rather than a controller.

Or

What are the different phases of a listening lesson? Give the plan of a listening lesson using a specific listening activity.

Q3. What are efficient reading skills? How can a teacher help in developing independent reading skills amongst his/her learners.

Or

What are the skills required for a meaningful oral interaction in the classroom? Mention ways in which you will develop these skills.

Q4. Describe the components of the communicative approach. Mention ways in which you will encourage learner autonomy and learner responsibility.

Or

Discuss how pair and group work can be used effectively in the classroom. However there are some aspects that need the teacher's attention. How can a teacher over come some of the problems of group activity?

Q5. Grammar is inextricably linked with meaning. Discuss this statement. Give examples to illustrate your answer.

Or

An effective teacher is one who is resourceful and not slavishly attached to the textbook. Discuss how a teacher can adapt materials to use in the English Class. Give examples to illustrate your answer.

TEACHING STRATEGIES: CTE-03
December, 2014

*Note: Attempt all questions. All questions carry **equal** marks.*

Q1. Write short notes on any four of the following:

Give examples whenever necessary.

(a) Characteristics of a spoken language

(b) Fluency versus Accuracy

(c) Ice breakers

(d) The process-oriented approach to teaching

(e) Using newspaper headlines for teaching communication skills

(f) Functional syllabus

Q2. Discuss the role of language games in a 'communicative' classroom. Also illustrate this with the help of two language games.

Or

Explain how you will teach modals to class VIII students keeping in view the following:

(a) Teaching grammar in realistic situations

(b) Teaching grammar as discourse

Q3. What is meant by efficient reading? Explain with examples the characteristics of efficient reading.

Or

Define the role of silent reading and reading aloud in the process of acquiring good reading skills. What kind of texts would you select for silent reading and reading aloud? Give reasons for selecting the texts.

Q4. Bring out the importance of simulation and role play in a language classroom with the help of activities. Also discuss the role of the teacher in such activities.

Or

What is the role of motivation in a language classroom? Discuss how you will use TV watching habit of children as a motivational strategy for language learning.

Q5. Discuss the importance of monitoring in the language classroom with illustrations from your own teaching-learning experience. What aspects should you monitor in your teaching context and how do you propose to do it?

Or

What is practitioner research? Why should a teacher be a researcher?

◈ ◈ ◈

TEACHING STRATEGIES: CTE-03
June, 2015

*Note: Attempt all questions. All questions carry **equal** marks.*

Q1. **Write short notes on any four of the following:**

Give examples wherever necessary.

(a) **Difference between Spoken and Written language**

(b) **Formal versus Informal style of writing**

(c) **Developing instructional materials**

(d) **Mixed ability group**

(e) **Practitioner Research**

(f) **Extensive and Intensive reading**

Q2. **Discuss the concerns about pair/group work in a language classroom. How can you overcome the limitations of pair/group work?**

Or

Why do discipline problems occur in a class? What can a teacher do to overcome them?

Q3. **What are the characteristics of spoken language? What do you understand by negotiation of meaning in the process of interaction?**

Or

Differentiate between the approaches of process writing and product writing. Which do you prefer keeping your teaching context in view? Also give examples to illustrate the difference.

Q4. **Differentiate between the skill-based and structural syllabus with examples of activities used wit each. Which one do you prefer and why?**

Or

What are ice-breakers? Give four ice-breaker activities that may be used in a language classroom. (Level–Class VI and VII)

Q5. **Discuss in detail the concepts of fluency and accuracy. What do you emphasise in your teaching context? Why?**

Or

Discuss the principles (four) of teaching writing with two activities under each principle, to exemplify the same.

TEACHING STRATEGIES: CTE-03
December, 2015

Note: Attempt all questions. All questions carry ***equal*** *marks.*

Q1. Write short notes on any four of the following:

(a) Characteristics of real-life listening situations

(b) Reading problems that learners face

(c) Simulation and role play in teaching spoken English

(d) Fluency and Accuracy in language learning

(e) How would you define grammar?

(f) Functional and Situational syllabi

Q2. What are the characteristics of reading? Explain the reading process in detail.

Or

What is the difference between intensive and extensive listening comprehension? Suggest the activities for the three phases of a listening lesson.

Q3. What are the different approaches to teaching grammar? How has the teaching of grammar changed in current times, and what is your opinion about it?

Or

What are the differences between spoken and written language? Explain the direct and indirect approaches to teaching conversation. Develop a lesson plan to teach students how to express agreement/ disagreement on any issue, using any approach you think suitable.

Q4. What are the different approaches to teaching writing? Develop a lesson plan to teach students how to write an analytical essay.

Or

What aspects of pronunciation would you teach and why? Explain how you would improve students' pronunciation, giving examples.

Q5. What is the main difference between internal and external evaluation of teaching materials? Why is it required? Support your answer by giving examples.

Or

Explain the difference between adopting and adapting materials. What methods would you use to 'adapt' a text that has very difficult vocabulary and is culturally alien?

◈◈◈

TEACHING STRATEGIES: CTE-03
June, 2016

*Note: Attempt all questions. All questions carry **equal** marks.*

Q1. Write short notes on any four of the following in about 150 words each:

(a) Schemata in reading comprehension

Ans. Refer to Chapter-2, Q.No.-9

(b) The difference between information and interaction routines in spoken English

Ans. Refer to Chapter-3, Q.No.-4

(c) The need for course books in language teaching/ learning

Ans. A textbook is necessary not only because it contains all the information required but also because it is a practical aid to the process of teaching and learning. The difference between a textbook and a general book on the same subject is merely this: the former is meant for a particular group and provides specific information whose limits have been predetermined, whereas the latter is meant for a general group **and seeks** to cover a much wider range of information and knowledge. Given a particular level of learning, the course book defines the limits of its area and gives as much information as is considered essential to the target group. It is no longer the teacher's job to decide how much. It is all laid down in the book.

From the learner's point of view, the course book is important in that she can go back to it any number of times for reinforcement, clarification and a better understanding of the content. What is taught by the teacher may have been learnt at that time, but one might have difficulty later in recalling the matter in all its details. The textbook is there to be studied all over again.

The course book is also important because it gives us a chance to learn through reading, which is one of the major skills in the learning process. That is why it is recommended that one's reading should not be confined to the course books alone. One should begin with the prescribed book, and given interest and inclination, transcend it to acquire deeper knowledge of the subject. Children who have learnt to read with comprehension should be encouraged to read poems and stories outside the course materials. Wide reading enlarges one's scope of understanding and appreciation. The course book do introduce us to the important skill of reading.

(d) Extensive and intensive listening comprehension

Ans. Refer to Chapter-2, Q.No.-6

(e) Reasons for reading in daily life

Ans. Some of the reasons of reading in our daily life are as follows:

(1) We want information for some purpose, or because we are curious to know about some topic, the answer to a question, or the solution to a problem;

(2) We need instructions in order to perform some task in our work or in our daily life (we want to know how an appliance works or how to make a model airplane, we are interested in a new recipe for baking a cake, we have to fill in forms);

(3) We want to keep in touch with friends through letters, or understand official correspondence;

(4) We want to know when or where something will take place or what is available (we consult timetables, programmes, announcements, notices, and menus, or we read advertisements);

(5) We want to know what is happening or has happened (newspapers, magazines, reports);

(6) We want to play a new game, do a puzzle, act in a play, or do some other activity which is pleasant, amusing and enjoyable;

(7) We seek enjoyment or excitement (short stories, novels, songs, and poems).

(f) Management of spoken interaction

Ans. This gives the participants in a conversation the freedom to choose the topic of conversation and develop it as they wish. It also gives them the right to choose how long a conversation should continue and to start and end a conversation when they wish to. The choice of topic, depends partly on the interest of the participants and is partly a matter of what is appropriate in the given context. For example, in casual conversation the choice of topic is much freer and can be changed more frequently by the participants than formal institutional talk. The latter is much more controlled and structured than the former and may be more difficult for the learner.

The second aspect *of* management of interaction is turn-taking. The speaker needs to know how to negotiate control of a conversation. She has to learn how to get a turn and let another speaker have a turn. In order to be efficient at turn taking one needs to know how to signal that one wants to speak, by using appropriate phrases or sounds or even gestures. For example, one way of doing this would be to start by agreeing with the previous speaker in some way and only then make a different point. One must also be able to recognise the right moment to *get* a turn, because an interruption at the wrong moment can at times sound very rude. Having got a turn, one must present what one has to say in a manner that will help one to retain one's turn until one has finished saying what one has to say. This can be done by using expressions such as "first" "another thing" "then" to suggest continuity. In addition to being efficient in getting one's turn and retaining it, one has also to recognise other people's signals of their desire to *speak* and to know how to let them have their turn.

Q2. What criteria should we adopt in selecting texts for intensive reading? Support your answer with example.

Ans. Refer to Chapter-2, Q.No.-17

Or

Which five sub-skills are common to both reading and listening? Suggest activities that you would do to develop these skills in your students.

Ans. Refer to Chapter-2, Q.No.-1 and Q.No.-18

Q3. What are the characteristics of spoken language? In your own teaching, do you emphasize fluency or accuracy? why?

Ans. Refer to Chapter-3, Q.No.-3 and Q.No.-7

Or

In the conventional classroom, listening and speaking skills tend to get ignored. Why? As a teacher, how would you ensure greater 'student talk'. Give examples of at least two activities.

Ans. In the conventional classroom, listening and speaking skills tend to get ignored. The student does not get opportunities to move about, talk, ask question, and so on. In the traditional textbooks, however, when the students are called upon to answer questions, they are often instructed to give only affirmative or negative answers or full or short answers. That cannot be counted as communication, since communication involves freedom and unpredictability.

As teachers, there is a need to create situations in a classroom where students can get an opportunity to respond to a particular situation with the help of language inputs which s/he **has** already mastered.

Now, Refer to Chapter-3, Q.No.-10

Q4. What is meant by the 'Communicative approach' to language teaching/learning? What are its main features?

Ans. Refer to Chapter-4, Q.No.-5

Or

What are the main objectives of a good reading programme? How would you develop inferencing skills in your students? Explain with examples.

Ans. Refer to Chapter-2, Q.No.-16 and Q.No.-18

Q5. What are the main approaches to teaching grammar? Which do you prefer and why? Explain with examples.

Ans. Refer to Chapter-3, Q.No.-16

I prefer the third approach, i.e. providing opportunities to use English in realistic situations because in this approach learners are given opportunities to engage in the process of communication; this will enable them to acquire the proficiency to communicate (which includes grammatical competence as well). In this approach, learners learn by doing, i.e. they learn to communicate by communicating, and not by mastering a set of rules or repeating a set of patterns. The basic essence of this approach is to primarily concentrate or communication, to the exclusion of grammar.

Or

What problems do your learners face in writing? Develop a lesson plan that aims to overcome these problems; taking letter writing as the basic activity.

Ans. Refer to June-2011, Q.No.-1(f)

To overcome of the problems which learner face in writing, a teacher can give various task on letter writing as lesson plan.

Task 1

Read the following letters carefully:

Letter A

________ 1 ________ ________ 2 ________

________ 3 ________

I regret to inform you that I lost a book which I borrowed from your library on 2 May 1986. The book is Oliver Twist by Charles Dickens.

As I am unable to trace it, I am willing to replace the book or pay the cost, according to your preference.

I sincerely apologise for my carelessness.

________ 4 ________

S. Rao

Letter B

________ 1 ________ ________ 2 ________

________ 3 ________

Do you remember that I borrowed a book from you when we met last? I think it was a novel by Dickens. I forget the title. Well, last Monday I was taking it to college. The bus was terribly crowded and I was actually standing on the feet of two other men. It was sheer relief when the bus reached college. I jumped out and went straight for a cup of coffee. Later, to my horror, I found that your book was missing.

I am awfully sorry, Hari. It was really foolish of me to have been so careless. Have you written your name and address on the book? Let's wait for a week and *see*. I'll also enquire at the bus depot. In case I don't find it, you should let me buy it for you. It's only fair, don't you agree?
Bye for the moment. Do write back.

4

Ram.

Now, answer the following questions:

(1) To whom is Rao writing his letter? How do you know?

(2) To whom is Ram writing his letter? How do you know?

(3) Now, can you fill in the boxes numbered 1,2,3 & 4 in both the letters?

(4) The purpose of both the letters is the same. What is it?

(5) Even though both the letters have the same purpose, they are written differently. Why?

(6) Why is Letter A much shorter than Letter B?

(7) Letter B has many items of information, which are not found in Letter A. (Example) "It was actually standing on the feet of two other men." Can you find any more items like this?

(8) There are a number of items of information common to A and B, but they are presented differently.

   (i) (eg.) Letter A - "I sincerely apologise for my carelessness."

   (ii) "Letter B - "I am awfully sorry, Hari. It was really foolish of me to have been so careless."

Pick out other parallel items.

(9) If Ram had written the same letter to a librarian what would be his reaction? Why?

(10) Fill in the table below:

Lettter A	**Letter B**
1. ____________	Personal letter
2. Brief	____________
3. Only relevant facts	____________
4. ____________	Informal language
5. ____________	Personal/friendly tone.

Task 2

Read the following letter:

My dear **Rajan,**

I am very unhappy and disappointed. You know, I can't go to Delhi. I had been selected to represent Madras at the National games. I was really excited; and believe it or not every morning I get up at four O'clock and run along the Marina. Well, yesterday as I was running, I saw a scooterist coming very fast towards me. Before I could collect my wits he ran over me, and just disappeared. Some kind old man who happened to be jogging on the road took pity on me and brought me to the hospital. Now I am down with a fracture of the thigh and cannot move for at least four weeks. And I really keep crying all the time for having missed the golden opportunity of my life. Could you please visit me sometime? I'm waiting for you.

Yours affectionately,

Sekhar

Rajan wrote another letter to the Physical Director of his college explaining that he would not be able to represent the college at the Delhi National Games. Can you write it for him?

Task 3

What is wrong with the following letter? Rewrite it properly.

Respected Sir, I am the ideal candidate for the post of a lecturer in your college.

I am' very anxious to get the job because my father has retired and I have to look after my parents.

If you appoint me, I am ready to do anything for you. I hope you will be kind enough to give me the job. Remember also that I have old parents to look after.

I have had an excellent education. I sing beautifully. You can **see** from this letter that my knowledge of English is perfect. Why should I waste your time with a long list of qualifications? We should talk about this at the interview.; I shouldn't bore you now.

Please have the interview soon. I need the job desperately.1 remain,

Your humble and went servant,

Seenu.

Task 4

Write an application in answer to the following advertisement in The Hindu dated 13th October 1985:

> WANTED SMART LADIES
> having good command in
> English for the posts of typists
> and account assistants. Salary no
> bar for deserving candiates.
> APPLY with complete details to
> Box No. 8847, C/O. The Hindu,
> Madras 600 002.

◈◈◈

TEACHING STRATEGIES: CTE-03
December, 2016

*Note: Attempt all questions. All questions carry **equal** marks.*

Q1. Write short notes on any four of the following:

Give examples wherever necessary.

(a) Teaching the main course book

(b) Cooperation and collaboration in the classroom

(c) Importance of developing listening skills

(d) Problems in teaching reading

(e) Developing fluency in speaking

(f) Simulation and role play

Q2. What are the essential features of good course materials? Illustrate with an example of the materials you have successfully used in your classroom.

Or

Teachers need to evaluate materials. Why? Which is more useful — internal evaluation or external evaluation? Why?

Q3. How would you define an efficient reader? What are the characteristic features of reading as a skill?

Or

What is the approach to teaching grammar that is followed today? What are the principles behind this approach? Outline any three principles of grammar teaching and give examples of their effectiveness.

Q4. Why are warm-up activities and ice-breakers essential? Write briefly about a few such activities you can use in your classroom. Describe any one of them in detail.

Or

Why do students need to be provided opportunities to communicate in the classroom? Describe any two language games and explain how you would use them to develop students' communication skills.

Q5. Why is self-monitoring important in teaching? How can it help in the professional growth of even the experienced teachers?

Or

Do you agree with Raimes who said, "We have to teach writing"? Give reasons. What are the problems in teaching writing that teachers of English face? What are your suggestions for overcoming these problems?

◈◈◈

TEACHING STRATEGIES: CTE-03
June, 2017

Note: Attempt all questions. All questions carry ***equal*** *marks.*

Q1. Write short notes on any four of the following.

Give examples wherever necessary.

(a) The importance of supplementary readers

Ans. Refer to Chapter-2, Q.No.-13

(b) Fluency vs Accuracy

Ans. Refer to Chapter-3, Q.No.-7

(c) Developing reading comprehension

Ans. Refer to Chapter-2, Q.No.-12

(d) Language games and activities

Ans. Refer to Chapter-3, Q.No.-8

(e) Role play and simulation

Ans. Refer to Chapter-3, Q.No.-11

(f) Problems in teaching writing

Ans. Refer to June-2011, Q.No.-1 (f)

Q2. Elaborate upon the different kinds of materials used in a language class. How can materials be adapted by practising teachers? Give examples.

Ans. Refer to Chapter-1, Q.No.-1

Or

Do you think English should be introduced in Class I or later? Give reasons for your answer and support your arguments with examples.

Ans. We know that in most parts of the country it is introduced in class VI as a second language. There are also many schools everywhere which start English in Class I. We are now thinking of a book which will be used in the first year of the English teaching programme. In other words, class VI will be class I as far as English is concerned.

We are teaching English to our students because it serves some important social and cultural functions. It prepares them for higher education in areas where knowledge is not available in our own languages. It has a rich literary tradition. It is a world language. It is the associate official language in our country. English, therefore, should be taught. Hence, there is a need of good textbooks. We need to study the teaching items specified in the syllabus. Since children haven't learnt to read with ease 4 yet, there is no point in giving them supplementary reading material. We can develop students' listening skills and improving their ability to learn a new sound system by an audio cassette, the alternate of textbook. That will be of great help.

The course book should not begin with connected texts. We follow the principle of progressive movement from simple to complex to more complex. They Should learn a certain number of words and phrases and should be able to write short and connected sentences at the end of the course. The socio-cultural milieu of the book is that it is meant for children living in villages and small towns, there should be references to the surroundings they are familiar with, the clothes they wear, and so on.

In our country teaching materials are produced by textbook Bureaus in the states. Boards of Education, national organisations like the National Council of Educational Research and Training (NCER'P), New Delhi, and Indira Gandhi National Open University (IGNOU), New Delhi, and by private authors and publishers. However, the situation regarding writing, printing, supply and distribution of textual materials varies from state to state. In some states, the work of curriculum development and text book preparation is combined. In some other states, books prepared by private publishers are also prescribed/recommended by the Boards of Secondary Education. The publishers submit their books to the Boards which generally follow certain criteria laid down for the scrutiny and approval of the books.

Q3. Grammar teaching has undergone great changes. Which approach to grammar teaching do you prefer – (a) giving students formal explanations of grammar rules or (b) providing students with opportunities to use English in realistic situations? Support your choice with examples.

Ans. Refer to Chapter-3, Q.No.-16

Or

Why is student interaction important in the classroom? Write about some of the techniques of interaction that can be used effectively to develop students' skills.

Ans. Refer to Chapter-3, Q.No.-4

Q4. Why should listening be taught? What are the listening situations students encounter in their day-to-day life? Elaborate upon some of these and show how they can be used to develop students into good listeners.

Ans. Refer to Chapter-2, Q.No.-1 and Q.No.-2

Or

What are 'enabling skills'? Elaborate upon the enabling skills required by students to develop their listening and reading skills.

Give examples wherever required.

Ans. The enabling skills are used to rate performance in the productive skills of speaking and writing. The enabling skills measured are grammar, oral fluency, pronunciation, spelling, vocabulary, and written discourse.

Now, Refer to Chapter-2, Q.No.-1 (Page No.-36)

Q5. What are the different approaches to teaching writing? Write about any one of them in detail.

Ans. Refer to Chapter-3, Q.No.-15

Or

What is the role of a teacher in communicative class? Write about some of the warm-up activities that a teacher can use in the classroom to effectively introduce a particular topic. Give examples.

Ans. Refer to Chapter-3, Q.No.-12 and Q.No.-10

TEACHING STRATEGIES: CTE-03
December, 2017

Note: Question no. 1 is compulsory. Answer any four questions from questions no. 2 to 7. You must answer five questions in all.

Q1. Write short notes on any *four* of the following. Give examples wherever necessary.

Distinguish between the following:

(a) Fluency and Accuracy

(b) Oral versus Written communication

(c) Information and Interaction routines

(d) Appropriacy and Authenticity

(e) Simulation and Role play

(f) Intensive and Extensive reading

Q2. What are the objectives of a Reading Programme? Discuss the enabling skills that help students to develop efficient reading techniques.

Q3. What are the different ways in which a teacher can monitor his/her teaching? How would that benefit his/her teaching and help in the teaching-learning process?

Q4. How would you develop listening comprehension of a learner? Provide a lesson plan for a listening skill class.

Q5. What do you understand by the process-oriented approach to writing? Provide activities you would undertake to help learners attempt a writing task.

Q6. If you were asked to select a textbook for your learners, what would be the criteria for your choice? Give a profile of your learners as well.

Q7. Discuss the role of the teacher in a Spoken Skills class. What is the difference between the Indirect and Direct approaches to teaching the Speaking Skill?

◈ ◈ ◈

TEACHING STRATEGIES: CTE-03
June, 2018

*Note: Attempt all questions. All questions carry **equal** marks.*

Q1. Write short notes on any four of the following in about 150 words each.

(a) Advantages of Pair and Group Work

Ans. Refer to Chapter-1, Q.No.-3

(b) Interpretive Reading

Ans. Refer to Chapter-2, Q.No.-14

(c) Differences between Spoken and Written Language

Ans. Refer to Chapter-3, Q.No.-2

(d) Different Aspects of Writing

Ans. Refer to Chapter-3, Q.No.-13

(e) Why Do We Need Course Books?

Ans. Refer to June-2016, Q.No.-1(c)

(f) Contexts for Reading Aloud

Ans. Refer to Chapter-2, Q.No.-9

Q2. In what ways is 'practitioner research' a part of 'good teaching'? Discuss giving examples.

Ans. Refer to Chapter-1, Q.No.-10

Or

Discuss pair work as part of effective classroom management in a large class.

Ans. Refer to Chapter-1, Q.No.-3

Q3. During the reading process, the reader and the writer, together create the meaning. And the constructed meaning is unique to the reader. Discuss in the context of the reading process.

Ans. Refer to Chapter-2, Q.No.-9

Or

Explain the different levels of reading comprehension.

Ans. Refer to Chapter-2, Q.No.-14

Q4. How would you create a need to communicate in the classroom? Discuss how you would use communicative games for this purpose. Provide examples.

Ans. Refer to Chapter-3, Q.No.-8

Or

What is Grammar? Discuss the different approaches to teaching grammar.

Ans. Refer to Chapter-3, Q.No.-17 and Q.No.-16

Q5. Explain the communicative approach in English language teaching. What is the role of the teacher and the materials under this approach?

Ans. Refer to Chapter-4, Q.No.-5

Or

If you were asked to select materials for your class, what would you look for? Discuss with reference to external and internal evaluation.

Ans. Refer to Chapter-4, Q.No.-6

◈ ◈ ◈

"Whatever the mind of man can conceive and believe, it can achieve".

- W. Clement Stone

TEACHING STRATEGIES: CTE-03
December, 2018

*Note: Attempt all questions. All questions carry **equal** marks.*

Q1. Write short notes on any four of the following. Give examples wherever necessary.

(a) Features of Satisfactory Course Material

Ans. Refer to Chapter-4, Q.No.-3 (Pg. No.-117)

(b) The Reflective Teacher

Ans. Refer to Chapter-1, Q.No.-9, Q.No.-10 and Q.No.-11 (Pg. No.-30, 31, 32)

(c) Use of Activities for Teaching Reading

Ans. Refer to Chapter-2, Q.No.-18 (Pg. No.-70)

(d) The Need for Teaching Listening Comprehension

Ans. Refer to Chapter-2, Q.No.-6 (Pg. No.-41)

(e) Different Approaches to Teaching Writing

Ans. Refer to Chapter-3, Q.No.-14 and Q.No.-15 (Pg. No.-104, 105)

(f) Difference between Direct and Indirect Approach to Teaching Speaking

Ans. Refer to Chapter-3, Q.No.-6 (Pg. No.-92)

Q2. Summarise the similarities and differences between spoken and written language.

Ans. Refer to Chapter-3, Q.No.-1 and Q.No.-2 (Pg. No.-82, 84)

Or

Discuss four communication games that can be used by the teacher to teach the spoken skill to young learners.

Ans. Refer to Chapter-3, Q.No.-10 (Pg. No.-98)

Q3. When developing materials for teaching English we must be conscious of the various types of syllabi involved. What are these?

Ans. Refer to Chapter-4, Q.No.-4 (Pg. No.-119)

Or

Write briefly on the "nature of the writing". Should writing be taught? Discuss.

Ans. Refer to Chapter-3, Q.No.-13 (Pg. No.-102)

Q4. To be an effective teacher it is important to acquire the skill of classroom management. In this context write about organising pair work and group work.

Ans. Refer to Chapter-1, Q.No.-3 (Pg. No.-7)

Or

In the teaching of reading, one moves from the mechanical skills of loud reading to reading for comprehension. What are the characteristics of reading?

Ans. Refer to Chapter-2, Q.No.-10 (Pg. No.-54)

Q5. Why is grammar important in the teaching of language? What are some of the approaches to teaching grammar?

Ans. Refer to Chapter-3, Q.No.-17 and Q.No.-16 (Pg. No.-107, 106)

Or

Is it important to evaluate course materials? What are the ways to evaluate the materials?

Ans. Refer to Chapter-4, Q.No.-6 (Pg. No.-123)

◈ ◈ ◈

The art of being wise is the art of knowing what to overlook.

TEACHING STRATEGIES: CTE-03
June, 2019

Note: *Attempt all questions. All questions carry* ***equal*** *marks.*

Q1. Write short notes on any four of the following:

(a) Group work in a communicative classroom

Ans. Refer to Chapter-1, Q.No.-3 (Pg. No.-7)

(b) Teaching of functional grammar

Ans. Functional grammar recognizes that all language is ideologically based, which means that the worldview of the speaker or writer is inherent in the text. Functional grammar differs from traditional grammar in that there is not one 'right' way to speak or write, however the grammatical and lexical choices the speaker or writer makes are dependent on the context. Teachers, for example, would make different grammatical and lexical choices when reflecting on the poor behaviour of the same student in these situations;

- at a party with very close friends
- a written end of year report
- a formal meeting with the principal, parents and student

Functional grammar improves student literacy because it makes explicit the appropriate genre, grammar and vocabulary for the task. It makes clear the distinction between spoken and written language and provides guidelines for students who are having difficulty shifting from language more at the spoken end of the literacy continuum to language more at the written end of the literacy continuum. It also supports students whose only access to formal standard Australian English is in the classroom. Functional grammar provides students and teachers with a meta language, a language to talk about language.

(c) Evaluation of course material

Ans. Refer to Chapter-4, Q.No.-6 (Pg. No.-123)

(d) Some principles of classroom management

Ans. Principles of classroom management—

(1) Planning and Preparation: The first principle is that effective classroom management must be planned especially in terms of transitions and potential disruptions. Consider the following suggestions:

- Names are power in the classroom. Address students by name. Access a seating chart ahead of time or prepare seating charts ahead of time; create name tents for each student to grab on their way into class and take to their desks or have students to create their own name tents on a piece of paper.

- Identify the common times for student disruptions and behaviors, usually at the start of the lesson or class period, when topics are changed, or at the wrap-up and conclusion of a lesson or class period.
- Be ready for the behaviors outside of the classroom that are brought into the classroom, especially at the secondary level when classes change. Plans to engage students immediately with opening activities ("Do nows", anticipation guide, entry slips, etc.) can help ease transitions into class.

(2) Quality Relationships: Second, effective classroom management is a result of relationships in the classroom. Teachers need to develop warm and responsive relations with students that have boundaries and consequences. Students understand that "It's not what we say that matters; it's how we say it."When students know that we believe in them, they will interpret even harsh-sounding comments as statements of care.

(3) School Environment: Third, effective management is supported by routines and structures that are embedded into the classroom environment.

Consider the following suggestions:

- Develop a routine with students at the start of class and at the end of class so that students know what to expect.
- Be effective when giving instructions by keeping them short, clear, and concise. Do not repeat directions over and over, but provide directions-written and or visual- for students to reference.
- Provide an opportunity for students to acknowledge understanding of the instruction given. Asking for students to hold a thumbs up or thumbs down (close to the body) can be a quick assessment before moving on.
- Designate areas in the classroom for student access so that they know where to grab a slip of paper or a book; where they should leave papers.

(4) Observation and Documentation: Finally, teachers who are effective classroom managers continuously observe and document their learning, reflect and then act on noticeable patterns and behaviors in a timely manner.

(e) Role of the teacher in a communicative classroom

Ans. Refer to Chapter-3, Q.No.-12 (Pg. No.-101)

(f) Reading as a cognitive activity

Ans. Reading was the ability to parse letters as words, phrases and sentences and interpret meaning from them. The course defined the core meaning of reading as "the activity by which we interpret language messages in written or printed form." It was suggested that readers need to able to decode words and comprehend the connection between them and that the relationship between decoding and comprehension was not additive but dependent, i.e., strong decoding skills cannot compensate for weak comprehension skills or vice versa.

We read text through a sequence of eye movements that involve fixations and sacchades. The eye is still in a fixation and information is extracted. During a sacchades, the eyes move to the next point of fixation.

Q2. Spoken English means communicating through the spoken mode." What are some ways by which spoken English can be taught? What are some of the principles to be kept in mind?

Ans. Refer to Chapter-3, Q.No.-8 and Q.No.-9 (Pg. No.-95)

Or

What do you mean by the reading process? Discuss some of the characteristics of reading.

Ans. Refer to Chapter-2, Q.No.-9 and Q.No.-10 (Pg. No.-49, 54)

Q3. Why is teaching material the most important component of the curriculum? What are the types of material used most often?

Ans. Refer to Chapter-4, Q.No.-1 (Pg. No.-114)

Or

What is implied by the multi-syllabus approach? Discuss the approach most commonly used in schools.

Ans. Materials designed on the basis of a multi-syllabus approach have now come into existence representing a coordination of different approaches. The multi-syllabus is now the most observable indicator of principles on which materials produced during recent years are based. Here are some statements taken from course books. They will give you an idea of a multi-syllabus approach. These statements have been taken from Material and Methods in ELT by Jo McDonough and Christopher Shaw, Blackwell, 1993,.

- "carefully structured multi-syllabus approach .. systematic development of all 4 skills .... emphasis on pronunciation, study skills and vocabulary learning .... authentic and semi-authentic reading and listening practice .... language for immediate communication.
- thorough, communicative practice of grammatical structures ... coverage of all the 4 skills .... comprehensive coverage of the English tense system.
- plenty of practice in 'core' grammatical structures and deals with language at a deeper level ....covers all the 4 skills. ..makes students think about the language they are using.

- proven multi-syllabus approach ... careful pacing.....allowance for different learning styles and teaching situations....authentic reading and listening material ...motivating range of up-to-date topics.
- focuses on the "real English" students will encounter and need to use in today's world ... regular grammar sections focus on important grammatical areas at sentence level and above ...wide cross-section of real texts promotes reading for pleasure as well as developing functional reading skills ...word study ... encourages students to be selective in their vocabulary building."

One notices in the statements above, elements like skills, grammatical sentences, vocabulary, learning styles, reading for pleasure, and word study. Each claims part of the mainstream communicative considerations but goes beyond that to include other elements. This combination is an indication of the enriched multi-syllabus approach to the designing of course materials. What it has achieved in specific terms is to endorse and practice a range of communicative criteria and at the same time promote practice in formal properties of the language.

Now, Refer to Chapter-4, Q.No.-5 (Pg. No.-121)

Q4. Role play and simulation have an important role to play in an activity based classroom. Discuss in detail the elements of role play keeping in mind the teacher's role.

Ans. Refer to Chapter-3, Q.No.-11 (Pg. No.-100)

Or

Discuss the current trends in teaching grammar. Do you think these are better than the traditional approaches?

Ans. Refer to Chapter-3, Q.No.-18 (Pg. No.-109)

Q5. What are some of the listening skills that need to be taught? Suggest two listening tasks to be used in the classroom.

Ans. Refer to Chapter-2, Q.No.-6 (Pg. No.-41)

Or

It is said that writing can be taught. If this is so, what are some of the suggested approaches to the teaching of writing.

Ans. Writing being such a complex process, one may wonder 'Can writing be taught?' Yes, it can be, not through a series of lectures on "how to write", perhaps; but through creating conditions favourable for 'learning to write' in the classroom.

The more important and relevant question is "Should writing be taught?"- in other words, why should we teach writing? Raimes (1983) lists three major purposes for teaching writing:

(a) People frequently have to communicate through writing.

(b) Writing helps our students to learn in two ways: it reinforces the grammatical structures, vocabulary and idioms that they have already learnt; it enables them to be adventurous with language and take risks.

(c) Writing helps to reinforce learning; the close relationship between writing and thinking makes it a valuable part of any language course.

Approaches of teaching of writing: There are some of the suggested approaches to the teaching of writing.

(1) The Traditional Approach: During the last decade, serious research has been undertaken in analysing and teaching composition. Prior to that, most teachers felt that writing need not be taught at all. Even those who did make an attempt to teach writing, mainly concentrated on the format or rules; in fact such an attitude continues to prevail in most Indian schools today. For example, if a teacher teaches letter writing, she tells her students about the layout of the letter - where the addresses are to be written, the salutation, the close, etc. But very little guidance is offered on how to write the body of the letter itself. Similarly for precis writing, the teacher gives a lecture on the rules of writing a precis.

In the traditional approach, the learner masters the 'rules' of letter-writing or precis writing; but she is not able to apply this knowledge to his/her own letters or summaries. She is confused when she gets back his/her composition with the award of a poor grade and a lot of red marks. On the other hand, this approach makes less demands on the teacher. She can conduct composition classes without any preparation. She simply walks into the classroom and sets an exercise for the learners. They write what they know or rather, what they do not know. And thus the vicious cycle of frustration and lack of motivation continues.

(2) The Model Based Approach: Here the pupils are provided with a model text. They analyse the elements of the text and then write a parallel passage. Models are very helpful to weak learners; they do not know how to write on their own, and the models provide them good support. However, bright pupils often feel unhappy with models since it gives them no scope for originality or creativity. Hence models have to W used judiciously. Originally, the models are presented first and the approach may be represented as follows:

Study the Model - Analyse the elements - Produce a parallel text.

We can make the approach more challenging for the pupils by adopting the following procedure:

Specify task → Let learners write what they can → Study Model → Compare with learner's writing → Revise

The presentation of the model, in the context of his/her own writing, especially after his/her initial struggle is sure to be much more meaningful and useful for the learner.

(3) The Process-Oriented approach: Writing is often regarded as a thinking process. A writer goes through various processes when she writes a piece of composition: thinking, organising ideas, considering the context, and redrafting. However, it is not a linear process as it is often assumed to be. It is a hierarchical process in which different events need not take place in a sequential order, for the writer moves back and forth. For instance, in the process of redrafting, she may stumble upon a new idea. Skilled writers do have a tentative plan, which keeps changing as they write.

In order to arrive at the final product - an essay, an article, etc. - good writers adopt various processes. They plan, generate ideas, &aft, read, raise and rewrite. Our learners will also learn to write better if we guide them through these various processes. The process approach is a learner-centred approach. It models the writing process rather than the written product. It involves the active participation of learners and focuses on how to write rather than what to write.

(4) The Interactive Approach: The major aim of language teaching is to develop in our learners the ability to communicate in English; and communication involves interaction. Unless there is interaction, we cannot have proper communication. To promote interaction, we have to make sure that there is lively attention and active participation by learners. Interactive activities may take the form of pair work, group work, etc. We could even design tasks where a learner interacts with a text, and works on his/her own. In the traditional classrooms we have only one type of interaction - where the teacher interacts with the whole class; this is highly teacher dominated, since learners are expected to speak only when the teacher asks them to do so.

Interactive tasks create a relaxed atmosphere in the classroom. Further learners do not feel lonely or threatened. They begin to enjoy composition classes. They learn from each other and work without a sense of inhibition. In the process of interacting they acquire fluency in communication. They also get practice in all the four skills - listening, speaking, reading and writing; or rather, they learn to write through listening, speaking and reading.

TEACHING STRATEGIES: CTE-03
June, 2020

Note: *(i) Attempt all questions. (ii) All questions carry equal marks.*

Q1. **Write short notes on any four of the following. Give examples wherever necessary:**

(a) **Similarities between reading and listening.**

(b) **Adapting materials for the English classroom.**

(c) **Communication games for effective teaching-learning.**

(d) **Skill based vs. structural syllabus.**

(e) **Teaching grammar 'in context'.**

Q2. **What is the importance of using good course material? What features make the material 'communicative and useful'? Give examples of some material (at least two) that you have created or could create and use successfully in the classroom.**

Or

Which approach to grammar teaching do you prefer—(a) giving students formal explanations of grammar rules or (b) providing students opportunities to use English by engaging them in games and activities? Why? Support your choice with examples from your own experience.

Q3. **Is it important to teach listening? Give reasons. What are the listening situations that students encounter in their day to day life? Show, how these situations can be used to develop students into good listeners.**

Or

What are the problems in teaching writing that you as a teacher of English face? What are your suggestions for overcoming these problems? What approaches to teaching writing do you think work best? Give examples and reasons.

Q4. **What is the role of a teacher in a communicative class? Write about some of warm up/pre reading activities or tasks that a teacher can use to motivate her learners.**

Or

What are the objectives of a reading development programme? What are the criteria to be kept in mind while selecting texts for developing intensive reading?

Q5. Compare the different approaches to teaching writing. Which one do you think is the best and why?

Or

What are the functions of spoken communication? To speak effectively students need the skills of (a) negotiating meaning and (b) managing interaction. Explain these in detail with examples of activities through which you would develop them.

TEACHING STRATEGIES: CTE-03
December, 2020

Note: *Attempt all questions. All questions carry equal marks.*

Q1. Write short notes on any four of the following in about 150 words each:

(a) Approaches to teaching of speaking

(b) Authenticity in materials

(c) Faculty reading habits

(d) The reflective teacher

(e) Teaching pronunciation

(f) Teaching grammar for communication

Q2. "Communication games serve the purpose of learner-teacher and learner-learner interaction leading to language generation and language use by them." Justify this statement with illustrations for speaking and writing.

Or

Write about the importance of role play as a warm up activity. Design a role play as communication activity for speaking in an authentic context.

Q3. "Teacher research is an instrument for reflective teaching." What is classroom research? How does it support the teacher for enhanced learning in the classroom?

Or

"Practitioner research is necessary for the teacher to change her ways of teaching for learning." Illustrate this your experience.

Q4. Can writing be taught? Explain, how writing as a skill and a process should be developed in learners. Provide at least four exemplar tasks for writing.

Or

What are enabling skills for learning listening? How can these subskills be developed in learners? Provide examples for each subskill.

Q5. Write a lesson plan for teaching speaking for Class IX giving objectives, processes and learning outcomes. Also comment on the need for planning a lesson before it is transacted.

Or

Describe, how pair work, group work and whole class should be designed and conducted. Illustrate each one of these with examples.

◈ ◈ ◈

TEACHING STRATEGIES: CTE-03
June, 2021

Note: *Question No. 1 is compulsory. Answer any four questions from question nos. 2 to 7. You have to answer five questions in all.*

Q1. Write short notes on any four of the following:

(i) Organising pair work and group work: advantages and problems.

(ii) Difference between extensive and intensive listening with examples.

(iii) Difference between skimming and scanning a text for reading with examples.

(iv) Features of good course materials with examples.

(v) Characteristics of spoken language.

(vi) The interactive approach to writing.

(vii) The communicative approach–its advantages.

Q2. What do you mean by the term 'Monitoring'? How does monitoring one's own class help in self-improvement of your teaching-learning abilities? Give an example of one such class where your consciously tried to monitor yourself.

Q3. What are the characteristics of reading? Describe some of the 'reading' problems which your students may face. Discuss strategies to overcome these problems.

Q4. When you prescribe a course book, how do you evaluate it both externally and internally?

Q5. Discuss the various approaches to writing. Which one do you feel would be the most effective in the classroom and why?

Q6. Describe the two approaches to the teaching of conversation. Which one do you prefer and why?

Q7. Adapt any lesson that you have taught for listening purposes. What was the most difficult aspect in your adaptation process? Give an example of any one activity that you adapted.

TEACHING STRATEGIES: CTE-03

December, 2021

Note: *Question no. 1 is compulsory. Answer any four questions from question nos. 2 to 7. You have to answer five questions in all.*

Q1. Write short notes on any four of the following:

(a) Differences between Spoken and Written Communication

(b) Four Stages of a Grammar Lesson

(c) Objectives of a Reading Programme

(d) Practitioner Research

(e) Characteristics of Spoken Language

(f) The Structural Syllabus

(g) Communicative Language Teaching

Q2. Describe the two approaches to the teaching of conversation. Which one do you prefer and why?

Q3. What are the four approaches to writing mentioned in the course? Which one would you suggest to a new teacher and why?

Q4. Reading comprehension is an active process. Discuss, using concepts such as 'Schema theory', 'Prediction' and so on.

Q5. As a teacher you are involved in selecting and prescribing textbooks for the students. Discuss the role of both internal and external evaluation in selecting a textbook. You may give examples from your experience, if possible.

Q6. How would you develop the listening comprehension of your students? Provide a plan for a listening skill class with two activities.

Q7. Why is the teaching of grammar important? What are the current trends in teaching grammar?